LIFE MANAGEMENT SKILLS I

reproducible activity handouts
created for facilitators

A sampler collection of...

assertion	risk taking
discharge planning	role satisfaction
emotion identification	self-awareness
exercise	self-esteem
goal setting	sleep
leisure	stress management
motivation	support systems
nutrition	time management
problem solving	values clarification

Kathy L. Korb-Khalsa, OTR/L   Estelle A. Leutenberg   Stacey D. Azok, OTR/L

WELLNESS REPRODUCTIONS & PUBLISHING, LLC
A Guidance Channel Company

©1993 Wellness Reproductions and Publishing, LLC • 800 / 669-9208 • FAX 800 / 501-8120 • http://www.wellness-resources.com

Our book is dedicated to Mitchell A. Leutenberg,
who made a difference.

THANKS TO. . .

Hareendra Adhvaryu, M.D.
Debbie Angle, OTR / L
Eunice Benchell
Beverly A. Beven, R.N.C., M.A.
Jeffrey M. Brooks, C.P.A.
Paul S. Dennis, NHA, CMACHCA
Ye-Fan W. Glavin, Ph.D.
Jan Hughes, M.S., R.D.
Mary Jane Kirbus, CTRS
Diane Klann
Kathy Klein
Arielle Liat Korb
Shayna Livia Korb
Lynne M. L. Yulish
Barbara Marlowe, L.S.W.
Susan Fording-Sharpnack, M.S.N., R.N.
Paul Slominski, R. N.
Victor M. Victoroff, M.D.
Rick Weissbrod
Debra Williams, OTR
Fran Zamore, M.S.W.

Clark County
Mental Health Services
Springfield, Ohio

College Hospital
Rehabilitation Services
Cerritos, California

Firelands Community Hospital
Psychiatric Services
Sandusky, Ohio

Lutheran Medical Center
Cleveland, Ohio

Meridia Huron Hospital
Rehabilitation Department
4 North Staff
East Cleveland, Ohio

The Ohio State University
Upham Hall
Columbus, Ohio

Research Medical Center
Kansas City, Missouri

Westbay Manor
Westlake, Ohio

SPECIAL THANKS TO. . .

John Bazyk, M.S., OTR / L
Patricia Clarkson
Pat Johnson

Lois G. Klein
Gary S. Okin, J.D.
Jo Hershey Selden

Laurelwood Hospital, affiliated with The Mt. Sinai Medical Center, Willoughby, Ohio

THANK YOU TO AMY LEUTENBERG BRODSKY . . .

our Wellness Reproductions and Publishing artist, whose creativity and skill as an illustrator, and experience with clients, continues to give the Life Management Skills books unique, humorous, and meaningful artwork, and whose insights from her clinical work offered guidance on the content as well. Amy Leutenberg Brodsky, LISW, received her Masters of Science in Social Administration from the Mandel School of Applied Social Sciences, Case Western Reserve University. Her art training was received at Kent State University where she achieved a BFA in Studio Art. She continues to pursue her career as an artist, as well as facilitating wellness with children and families in crisis.

FOREWORD

The inspiration for our LIFE MANAGEMENT SKILLS books originated from an ongoing practical need observed within a mental health setting. Handouts had been typically used in treatment as a launching pad for activities, an organizational tool, a visual aid, a tangible reminder of information presented, and as a method for building rapport. However, available handouts often did not meet necessary, high-quality standards in content desired, format, appearance and organization – and lacked permission for reproduction.

We have attempted to meet these standards by offering this sampler collection of handouts which are highly reproducible, organized in a logical manner, designed for specific well-defined purposes, and activity-based, allowing for extensive client involvement. The graphic representations are intentionally different from handout to handout in typestyle, art and design to increase visual appeal, provide variety and clarify meaning.

LIFE MANAGEMENT SKILLS handouts are adaptable and have a broad usage enabling therapists, social workers, nurses, teachers, psychologists, counselors and other professionals to focus on specific goals with their specified populations.

The book has been designed to offer reproducible handouts on the front of each page and nonreproducible facilitator's information on the reverse side. The Facilitator's Information Sheet includes the following sections: Purpose, General Comments and Possible Activities.

We specifically chose spiral binding to allow for easier and accurate reproduction, an especially white paper for clear, sharp copies, and a heavier paper stock for its durability and opacity. If adaptations to any of the handouts are desired, it is recommended to make one copy of the handout, include the changes which will meet *your* specific needs, and then use this copy as the original.

We hope that you will find these handouts in LIFE MANAGEMENT SKILLS I fun, innovative and informative. We wish you much success with your therapeutic and educational endeavors and hope we can continue to be of assistance. Remember . . . creative handouts will hopefully generate creative activities and contribute to a greater sense of WELLNESS!

Wellness Reproductions and Publishing, LLC

Kathy L. Korb-Khalsa   *Estelle A. Leutenberg*

WELLNESS REPRODUCTIONS AND PUBLISHING, LLC

is an innovative company which began in 1988. As developers of creative therapeutic and educational products, we have a strong commitment to the mental health profession. Our rapidly growing business began by authoring and self-publishing the book LIFE MANAGEMENT SKILLS I. We have extended our product line to include group presentation posters, therapeutic games, skill building cards, EMOTIONS© identification products, LIFE MANAGEMENT SKILLS II, III, IV, V, VI, SEALS (Self-Esteem and Life Skills) books and corresponding cards, Self-Reflections and Images of Wellness Print series and educational products about serious mental illness. Our books are created with feedback from our customers. Please refer to the last page of this book, our "FEEDBACK" page, and let us hear from YOU!

P.O. Box 760 • Plainview, New York 11803-0760 • 800 / 669-9208 • FAX: 800 / 501-8120
e-mail: info@wellness-resources.com • website: http://wellness-resources.com

TABLE OF CONTENTS

Page numbers are on the Facilitator's Information Sheet, located on the reverse side of each handout.

DON'T FALL IN THE TRAP.....
ASK – DON'T ASSUME!

You have the **right** to ask questions!!

SITUATION	YOUR ASSUMPTION	YOU ASK	POSSIBLE RESPONSE(S)
Friends were supposed to meet you at 6 o'clock but they arrive an hour late.	1. They got in a car accident. 2. They stood me up. 3. They ran out of gas.	Why were you late?	1. We had a flat tire. 2. We got lost. 3. We <u>said</u> we'd be here at 7 o'clock.
You asked to borrow the car for Saturday night and your parent says NO!			
A police car pulls you over and stops you!			
You leave your teenagers home alone for the evening. When you walk in, you smell cigarette smoke!			

DON'T FALL IN THE TRAP.....

ASK – DON'T ASSUME!

I. PURPOSE:

To increase assertive skills by encouraging "asking" and discouraging "assuming."

II. GENERAL COMMENTS:

The trap of ASSUMING and not ASKING frequently gets people into uncomfortable situations. Often, incorrect assumptions are made. ASKING requires thought, time, and practice and will result in increased assertiveness.

III. POSSIBLE ACTIVITIES:

A. 1. Use the example provided to explain the concept.

   2. Encourage the group members to fill in the blank boxes.

   3. Encourage role-playing for the remaining situations.

   4. Process the right to ask questions and possible benefits.

B. 1. Divide the group into teams of 3 members. Member #1 writes reply in "Your Assumption" column and passes it to member #2 who writes reply in "You ask" column and passes it to member #3 who writes reply in "Possible Responses" column.

   2. Instruct members to rejoin the entire group.

   3. Encourage each team to share one or two favorites.

Aggressive • **ASSERTIVE** • Passive

Meet
AGNES AGGRESSIVE:

**I'm loud, bossy and pushy.
I dominate and intimidate people.
I violate other's rights.
I "get my way" at anyone's expense.
I "step" on people.
I react instantly.**

Meet
ALICE ASSERTIVE:

I'm firm, direct and honest.
I respect the rights of others and recognize the
importance of having my needs and rights
respected. I speak clearly and to the point.
I'm confident about who I am.
I realize I have choices about my life.

Meet
PATSY PASSIVE:

I'm unable to speak up for my rights.
(I don't even know what my rights are!)
I get "stepped on" often.
I'm meek, mild-mannered and very accommodating.

Aggressive • **ASSERTIVE** • Passive

I. PURPOSE:

To recognize these three types of communication styles.

To increase awareness of the advantages of being assertive.

To recognize how these styles present themselves in women.

II. GENERAL COMMENTS:

This is an overview of the three basic communication styles, including nonverbal communications, view of rights, and implications of these behaviors. Communication is most effective when assertive.

III. POSSIBLE ACTIVITIES:

A. Pursue discussion of the socialized role of women to be passive from childhood to adolescence to adulthood, and the consequences. (This is a particularly good handout for a women's group.)

B. This activity is designed to be used in conjunction with page 3 when both men and women are in the group. Divide group into 2 teams.

1. Instruct volunteers from team #1 to role-play one style and team #2 to guess which style was being presented.

2. The teams can repeat the process with team #2 role-playing and team #1 guessing.

3. Continue alternating.

PASSIVE   ASSERTIVE   **AGGRESSIVE**

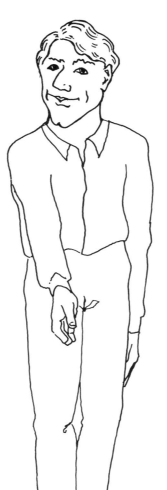

PASSIVE   ASSERTIVE   **AGGRESSIVE**

I. PURPOSE:

To recognize these three types of communication styles.

To increase awareness of the advantages of being assertive.

To recognize how these styles present themselves in men.

II. GENERAL COMMENTS:

This is an overview of the three basic communication styles, including nonverbal communications, view of rights, and implications of these behaviors. Communication is most effective when assertive.

III. POSSIBLE ACTIVITIES:

A. Pursue discussion of the socialized role of men to be aggressive from childhood to adolescence to adulthood, and the consequences. (This is a particularly good handout for a men's group.)

B. This activity is designed to be used in conjunction with page 2 when both men and women are in the group. Facilitate role-playing of the 3 communication styles using the following examples:

1. A friend needs to borrow $100.

2. You want a raise.

3. Your spouse has been away from home too much.

4. You're waiting at a restaurant for a half-hour and no one is helping you.

SAYING "NO"

YOU HAVE THE RIGHT TO SAY NO!

DO YOU HAVE TROUBLE SAYING "**NO**" TO....

_____ A. your mother? *(e.g., who continuously needs rides to the doctor/pharmacy/beauty salon)* _____

_____ B. door to door people? *(e.g., Girl Scouts selling cookies/salespeople/fundraisers/ religious enthusiasts/charity solicitors)* _____

_____ C. a friend? *(e.g., who wants you to use drugs/alcohol with him or her/wants to borrow money)* _____

_____ D. a neighbor? *(e.g., who wants you to watch her five children "just for an hour")*
_____

_____ E. your children? *(e.g., who want...new toys/more allowance/the car)*
_____

_____ F. a fellow worker? *(e.g., asks you to help him fix his car/go shopping with her/ contribute for a gift)* _____

_____ G. your spouse? *(e.g., who wants to buy his or her "dream car" which you feel is too much money at this time)* _____

_____ H. your boss? *(e.g., asking you to stay late)* _____

_____ I. _____ .

_____ J. _____ .

GUIDELINES TO SAYING "NO":
Be honest, open and direct.
Don't make excuses.
By saying "no" you're gaining self-respect.

EXAMPLE FORMATS...
No, I am unable to do that today. Maybe you can...
No...to be honest, I don't want to...

SAYING "NO"

I. PURPOSE:

To increase assertiveness by recognizing certain situations in which it is difficult to say "no," and rehearsing and listening to "no" in an assertive style.

II. GENERAL COMMENTS:

A nonassertive communication style often results in a reluctant "yes," a mixed message, and/or a hostile "no."

III. POSSIBLE ACTIVITIES:

A. 1. Instruct group members to read the situations and rank them from easy to difficult (1–9).

2. Discuss.

3. Review guidelines and example formats.

4. Role-play.

B. 1. Review handout.

2. Distribute strips of paper and have members write personal examples in which they have difficulty saying "no." Put in "hat."

3. Ask members to choose one and role-play.

R̶x for Wellness

☐ Exercise _____X Daily

Details: _____

_____

☐ Medications: _____

_____

_____

☐ Precautions: _____

☐ Community resource: Name _____

Address: _____

Phone number: _____ Meeting time: _____

Contact person's name: _____

☐ For emergency call: _____

Phone number(s): _____

☐ Dietary Recommendations: _____

_____

☐ Reminders: _____

_____

_____

_____

Team Member(s): _____

_____

Ŗ for Wellness

I. PURPOSE:

To increase responsibility of client or family for follow-up.

To receive information in a usable format and increase likelihood that information will be used for follow-up.

II. GENERAL COMMENTS:

Team members often provide valuable information to the client during the treatment process. It's important that it be offered in a centralized, organized, easy-to-read manner for hopeful carry-over with after-care, leaves of absence, post discharge, etc.

III. POSSIBLE ACTIVITIES:

A. 1. Instruct the client to fill in all relevant information seeking appropriate resources, e.g., P.D.R., telephone book(s), different team members, community resource guide.

2. Process importance of information and follow-through.

B. 1. Offer this handout in discharge-planning group, individual sessions, and at family meetings and provide help as needed for completion.

2. Encourage individuals to share at discharge-planning group prior to discharge.

Medication Reminder

BRAND NAME DRUG	GENERIC EQUIVALENT	FREQUENCY	TIMES	DOSAGE	COMMENTS
1.					
2.					
3.					
4.					
5.					
6.					
7.					
8.					
9.					
10.					

Pharmacy's Name _____   Phone _____

Doctor's Name _____   Phone _____

Other _____   Phone _____

# Medication Reminder

I. **PURPOSE:**

To increase responsibilities of client and/or family for medication compliance.

To increase knowledge of medications.

To receive this information in an organized form.

To increase likelihood that information will be used post discharge.

II. **GENERAL COMMENTS:**

It is helpful to have written details regarding medications for clients and their families and to offer it in a centralized, organized, and easy-to-read manner.

III. **POSSIBLE ACTIVITIES:**

A. Instruct the client to fill in all relevant information with the help of facilitator and/or staff. Possible remarks in the "comments" section may include:

1. main effects

2. possible side effects

3. where the medications are located

4. description of medications, e.g., color, size, tablet, capsule

B. Encourage group members to bring completed handout to discharge planning group or medication information group and...

1. discuss any concerns for post discharge.

2. discuss importance of medication compliance, what to do if running out of medications or noticing an increase in side effects, etc.

eMotIONS

aggressive	alienated	angry	annoyed	anxious	apathetic	bashful
bored	cautious	confident	confused	curious	depressed	determined
disappointed	discouraged	disgusted	embarrassed	enthusiastic	envious	ecstatic
excited	exhausted	fearful	frightened	frustrated	guilty	happy
helpless	hopeful	hostile	humiliated	hurt	hysterical	innocent
interested	jealous	lonely	loved	lovestruck	mischievous	miserable
negative	optimistic	pained	paranoid	peaceful	proud	puzzled
regretful	relieved	sad	satisfied	shocked	shy	sorry
stubborn	sure	surprised	suspicious	thoughtful	undecided	withdrawn

I. PURPOSE:

To increase awareness of emotions and a variety of words to express emotions, with assistance of visual representations.

To increase usage of these words.

II. GENERAL COMMENTS:

Identifying emotions is an effective communication skill. Everyday language can be enhanced by using the most specific word to describe feelings at any time. This allows the "receiver" to get a clearer picture of what the "sender" is trying to say and increases the chance of a more effective response.

III. POSSIBLE ACTIVITIES:

A. 1. Discuss with group members the concept of emotion identification and demonstrate variety through reference to handout.

2. Instruct each group member in sequence to select an emotion from the handout and share it with the group using one of the following formats:

"I feel _____ when _____."

or

"The last time I _____ was when _____."

3. Encourage all group members to check off the emotions from the handout as they are shared, so they will not be repeated.

4. Encourage this process to continue until all emotions are discussed from the handout.

B. 1. Make a card game by cutting each of the 63 emotions out of one handout and attach each on a separate index card. Place in a "hat."

2. Divide group into two teams.

3. Encourage one group member from team #1 to choose a card and pantomime the emotion for team #2. Then team #2 guesses which emotion it is. This handout can be given to all group members to assist them.

4. Score by giving one point for correct response given within 60 seconds.

5. Repeat process with team #2 pantomiming for team #1.

6. Continue game until time runs out or all cards are played.

7. Process the importance of using specific words to express emotions.

"I feel..."

... two very powerful words when used together to assert yourself. Personal power is lost when *"you make me feel"* is verbalized or implied. Taking ownership of your feelings allows you to make your needs known without violating the rights of others.

Make a list of common situations in which you give up control by blaming others for your feelings. Then try out the situation using this suggested approach beginning with "I feel". Recognize how accepting responsibility for your feelings will change your perception.

"You make me (feel)..."	"I feel..."	"Since I'm in control of my feelings, my choices are..."
You make me feel uncomfortable at parties when you drink.	*I feel uncomfortable at parties when you drink.*	*I can go and be miserable/turn my attention to others/leave the party/not go to the next one.*
You make me angry when you don't listen.	*I feel angry when you don't listen.*	*I can continue "as is" with resentment/ask you to set a specific time to talk/ask you to give some response (nod, eye contact, "okay").*

"I feel..."

I. PURPOSE:

To increase emotion identification by gaining experience and knowledge using "I feel" statements.

To recognize options as a result of being in control.

II. GENERAL COMMENTS:

Increased control and responsibility are felt when one states "I feel." "You make me feel" is a communication "bad habit" which gives control to the other person. "I feel" is in essence stating "I choose or allow myself to feel," thus giving increased choices to the individual.

III. POSSIBLE ACTIVITIES: This handout may be used in conjunction with EMOTIONS (page 7).

A. 1. Explain concept of handout by reading top portion of handout and two examples.

2. Encourage group members to complete page using personal examples.

3. Discuss and encourage members to share as able.

4. Process the use of "I feel" as one assertive principle.

B. 1. Distribute slips of paper and encourage each group member to jot down three personal examples of situations in which they have said "You make me feel." Place in "hat."

2. Instruct group members to choose one.

3. Encourage role-playing of each chosen situation.

4. Process benefits of assertive expression of feelings.

Exercise Record

Name _____   **Month** _____

	EXERCISE	TIME START	TIME END	TOTAL TIME	COMMENTS
1					
2					
3					
4					
5					
6					
7					
8					
9					
10					
11					
12					
13					
14					
15					
16					
17					
18					
19					
20					
21					
22					
23					
24					
25					
26					
27					
28					
29					
30					
31					

Exercise Record

I. PURPOSE:

To establish a record-keeping system promoting a commitment to exercise.

II. GENERAL COMMENTS:

Although most people realize exercise is of benefit, it is difficult to make a commitment to it. This handout enables people to visualize their accomplishments, which serves as motivation to continue.

III. POSSIBLE ACTIVITIES:

A. 1. Explain concept of record keeping.

    2. Instruct group members that "COMMENTS" section may include:

       a. pulse rate before and/or after exercise

       b. physical response before and/or after exercise

       c. emotional response before and/or after exercise

    3. Process benefits of record keeping.

B. 1. Explain concept of record keeping.

    2. Instruct group members that "COMMENTS" section may include:

       a. pulse rate before and/or after exercise

       b. physical response before and/or after exercise

       c. emotional response before and/or after exercise

    3. Discuss benefits of exercise.

    4. Assign homework to be completed by next session as follows:

       a. Write down all exercises (or lifestyle changes) within the time allotted.

       b. Bring back to the next group session.

    5. Collect papers and read aloud encouraging group members to guess who wrote each one.

    6. Process benefits of record keeping.

EXERCISE INTEREST CHECKLIST

It is well known that exercise is of benefit to everyone. Choosing which exercise to do is not an easy task! It depends on present physical condition, doctor recommendations (if necessary), personal likes and dislikes, etc.

Here's a list of choices. Put a "**P**" (present) in the first box if you presently do this two or more times each week. Put an "**F**" (future) in the second box if you are going to continue doing this or are considering doing this one or two times each week in the future.

☐☐	Jogging	☐☐	Bowling	☐☐	Baseball / Softball
☐☐	Walking	☐☐	Yardwork	☐☐	Roller / Ice-Skating
☐☐	Running	☐☐	Tennis	☐☐	Soccer
☐☐	Swimming	☐☐	Golf	☐☐	Volleyball
☐☐	Bicycling	☐☐	Weight Lifting	☐☐	Football
☐☐	Dancing	☐☐	Stretching	☐☐	Basketball
☐☐	Aerobics	☐☐	Aquatics	☐☐	_____
☐☐	Downhill Skiing	☐☐	Yoga	☐☐	_____
☐☐	Cross Country Skiing	☐☐	Work-out Machines	☐☐	_____
☐☐	Water Skiing	☐☐	Racquetball	☐☐	_____

List of "P"s

_____

_____

_____

_____

List of "F"s

_____

_____

_____

_____

List 3 "**F**"s that you are not doing presently and identify what you'll need to do to GET STARTED.

1. _____

2. _____

3. _____

EXERCISE INTEREST CHECKLIST

I. PURPOSE:

To take an inventory of present exercises and choose possible future exercises.

II. GENERAL COMMENTS:

Choosing the "right" exercise might be assisted by *reviewing* exercise choices, *selecting* realistic possibilities, and *discovering* what resources are available.

III. POSSIBLE ACTIVITIES:

A. 1. Present handout as indicated.

   2. Encourage group members to summarize their "P"'s and "F"'s and the resources where they can find "F"'s.

   3. Discuss and process benefits of choosing the "right" exercise regimen.

B. 1. Present handout as indicated.

   2. Encourage group members to brainstorm and make a list of possible facilities that offer the activities listed.

   3. Divide list among group members and instruct each to call the facility to determine costs, times of day offered, location, and other information.

   4. Instruct members to bring information back to the next meeting and share.

Fitness includes making lifestyle changes

All of us have room to make some "lifestyle changes" to improve fitness. Here are some practical ideas that might be incorporated into your daily routine.

(✔) Check those that you will consider. (If in doubt, check with your therapist or doctor.)

☐ Climbing stairs instead of using the elevator or escalator.

☐ Parking in the furthest spot in the parking lot and walk or jog to where you're going.

☐ Exercising at red lights when driving by using isometrics.

☐ Walking your dog or a neighborhood dog around the block regularly.

☐ Riding a bike: to work, to the store or to visit your friends.

☐ Walking or jogging: to work, to the store or to visit your friends.

☐ Stretching in bed, in the morning or evening, while listening to the radio.

☐ Doing housework or yardwork while wearing wrist or ankle weights.

☐ Other: _____

☐ _____

☐ _____

```
Fitness
includes
making
lifestyle
changes
```

I. PURPOSE:

To increase fitness awareness by presenting and exploring options in making lifestyle changes.

II. GENERAL COMMENTS:

Fitness is one important aspect of wellness. Basic lifestyle habits can be modified to improve fitness, but are often overlooked. This handout may be used in conjunction with EXERCISE RECORD (page 9).

III. POSSIBLE ACTIVITIES:

A. 1. Present concept of making lifestyle changes, why they are important, the benefits, etc.

2. Encourage group members to complete handout.

3. Discuss various options.

4. Pursue "other" category with ideas contributed by members.

5. Process the impact of making lifestyle changes.

B. 1. Write the letters of the alphabet on a chalkboard.

2. Encourage group members to choose one letter and offer a possible lifestyle change beginning with that letter.

3. Continue calling on group members in sequence to share examples until all 26 letters are utilized.

4. Process the impact of making lifestyle changes.

GOAL SETTING is one way to organize yourself and to get yourself moving in a positive direction.

Must be...

REALISTIC &

MEASURABLE

Can be...

Career-oriented
Personal
Financial
Social
Educational
Other

Include...

1. What goal you really want to accomplish.

_____ .

2. How you will evaluate/measure your progress.

_____ .

3. How much time it will take to reach this goal.

_____ .

GOAL SETTING is one way to organize yourself...

I. **PURPOSE:**

To increase knowledge about goals and benefits of goal setting, and learn to apply this information.

II. **GENERAL COMMENTS:**

Setting goals and ultimately achieving them gives a sense of direction or control to an individual which can lead to increased self-esteem.

III. **POSSIBLE ACTIVITIES:**

A. 1. Review content of handout with group members.

    a. CAN BE section—goals can be any combination of right-hand and left-hand columns, e.g., professional long-term, educational short-term.

    b. The terms short-term, long-term, and very long-term are subjective and relative terms depending on the population.

    c. INCLUDE section provides a framework of 3 different criteria to include in every goal.

2. See GOAL SETTING PRACTICE SHEET (page 13).

B. 1. Write the following words on index cards: realistic, measurable, professional, personal, financial, social, educational, short-term, long-term, very long-term, and any others you choose to add.

2. Encourage each member to choose a card and define the term in his own words.

3. Process benefits of goal setting.

Goal Setting
Practice Sheet

INCLUDE:
{
the **task or objective** you want to accomplish.
how it will be measured or what **standard or target** will be reached.
time span.
}

EXAMPLES:
{
I will *finish my GED,* with *70% marks* by *next year at this time.*
  (task)   (standard)   (time span)

I will *give up smoking* by *not smoking any cigarettes* for *one month.*
       (task)   (standard)   (time span)
}

YOUR TURN:

#1 _____

Can I really achieve this? *(realistic)*   YES ☐   NO ☐
How will I know when I've achieved this? *(measurable)*

#2 _____

Can I really achieve this? *(realistic)*   YES ☐   NO ☐
How will I know when I've achieved this? *(measurable)*

#3 _____

Can I really achieve this? *(realistic)*   YES ☐   NO☐
How will I know when I've achieved this? *(measurable)*

Goal Setting

Practice Sheet

I. **PURPOSE:**

To practice "goal setting" by learning to use the 3 necessary criteria as indicated on top portion of this handout.

II. **GENERAL COMMENTS:**

It takes practice to write realistic and measurable goals. Examples are included as a visual tool and reminder, but there are many other formats which are correct as long as they include the 3 criteria.

III. **POSSIBLE ACTIVITIES:** This handout can be used in conjunction with GOAL SETTING IS ONE WAY . . . (page 12) and/or GOALS (page 14).

A. 1. Encourage group members to complete handout with pencil (if goal is not realistic it can be erased and rewritten).

2. Allow group members to take turns reading their goals aloud, giving time for each to receive feedback.

3. Process need for goal setting, writing the goals, and strategically placing them as a positive reminder.

B. 1. Encourage group members to brainstorm possible goals on the chalkboard.

2. Address each goal one at a time, considering the 3 criteria.

3. Process need for goal setting, writing the goals, and strategically placing them as a positive reminder.

G⊙ALS

REALISTIC · MEASURABLE

Name _____

G⊙AL _____
_____
_____
_____
_____
_____

G⊙AL _____
_____
_____
_____

G⊙AL _____
_____
_____
_____

G⊙AL _____
_____
_____

G⊙AL _____
_____
_____

G⊛ALS

I. PURPOSE:

To encourage goal setting.

II. GENERAL COMMENTS:

Writing goals, rather than just verbalizing them, is one way of increasing the likelihood of follow-through.

III. POSSIBLE ACTIVITIES:

A. 1. Review goal setting information from pages 12 and 13.

2. Encourage group members to write 5 goals.

3. Instruct group members to choose one goal from their handouts and write it on the chalkboard eliciting feedback from others.

4. Process benefits of goal setting.

5. Encourage group members to place their goal sheets in a highly visible location to serve as a motivator.

B. This handout may be reproduced to include 2 goals per page or 8 goals per page, simply by:

a. reproducing this page as is

b. cutting in half and pairing it with another half *(see illustrations below)*

c. reproducing desired amount

d. cutting in half, if desired

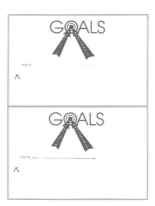

ONE STEP AT A TIME!

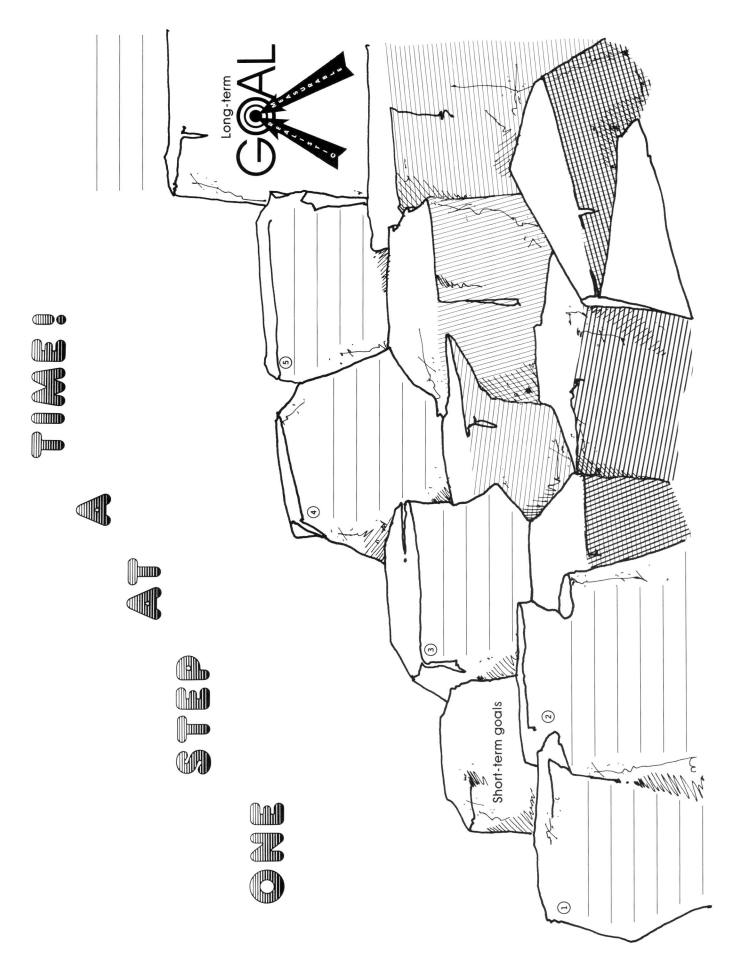

Short-term goals

① ② ③ ④ ⑤

Long-term GOAL

REALISTIC MEASURABLE

ONE STEP AT A TIME!

I. PURPOSE:

To gain an understanding regarding the importance of short-term goals in meeting long-term goals.

To gain experience in identifying and writing realistic short-term goals.

II. GENERAL COMMENTS:

Short-term goals can be viewed as "stepping stones" enabling one to meet a long-term goal. One way of recognizing progress toward a long-term goal is by acknowledging achievement of short-term goals.

III. POSSIBLE ACTIVITIES:

A. 1. Instruct group members to write their long-term goal on the right-hand top 3 lines. The following example may be used: finish high school or get my GED.

2. Encourage group members to write the first thing needed to be done in order to meet that long-term goal. They should write this in stone #1 (*find out where GED classes are held*). Proceed to stone #2 (*telephone them to get details*), stone #3 (*pick the best location for me*), stone #4 (*register*), and stone #5 (*go to classes and pass the course!*).

3. Ask group members to share their example and elicit feedback.

4. Process the value of short-term goals in conjunction with long-term goals.

B. 1. Give one stapled packet of 6 handouts to each group member.

2. Assign the following categories as goal topics:

    a. professional

    b. personal

    c. financial

    d. social

    e. educational

    f. other

3. Instruct group members to complete one handout per category. Educational goals stated in A.2. may be used as an example.

4. Request that all group members bring the packet back to the group and share them during the next session.

5. Process the value of short-term goals in conjunction with long-term goals.

LEISURE VALUES

Leisure Activity	Alone	With Others	Inside	Outside	Active	Passive	Challenging	Risky	Relaxing	Funny	Serious	Thought-Provoking	Competitive	Diversional	Self-Development	Cultural	Creative	Meaningful	Other

How do your present leisure **habits** compare to your leisure **values**?

_____

_____

_____

_____

_____

_____

What is one new leisure activity you will get involved in that incorporates some of these values?

_____

LEISURE VALUES

I. PURPOSE:

To identify values regarding leisure by analyzing qualities of activities.

To identify present leisure habits and compare them to leisure values.

II. GENERAL COMMENTS:

It is important to be aware of the reasons certain leisure activities are enjoyed so that efforts can be made to continue having satisfying experiences. Oftentimes, people say that they value certain types of activities yet do not engage in these. Leisure habits may be modified if needed to include values and increase satisfaction.

III. POSSIBLE ACTIVITIES:

A. 1. Explain concept of balancing work, **leisure**, and self-care activities.

2. Instruct group members to complete handout by identifying 6 leisure activities they enjoy: past and present.

3. Next ask them to check all qualities that "attract" them to each of these activities.

4. Encourage them to write a narrative response describing the differences/similarities between their leisure habits and their leisure values and answer remaining questions on handout.

5. Facilitate discussion regarding insights and process benefits of leisure involvement.

B. 1. Write each of the 18 listed leisure qualities on separate index cards and shuffle.

2. Instruct group members to take turns choosing a card and identifying one leisure activity they enjoy which has that quality. Continue until all 18 are discussed.

3. Facilitate discussion regarding insights and process benefits of leisure involvement.

LEISURE WITHOUT LOSS . . .

. . . of $ $ $ that is!

Wellness! A balance of work, **leisure**, and self care activities is one requirement for wellness.

Money is often a concern when engaging in leisure activities. Many leisure opportunities cost a great deal, but not all! Some of the most enjoyable experiences are free!

List below free (or almost free) leisure opportunities available to you.

_____   _____
_____   _____
_____   _____
_____   _____
_____   _____
_____   _____
_____   _____
_____   _____

Put a star (✳) by the five you will pursue.

How can you make these part of your life? _____

_____
_____
_____
_____

LEISURE WITHOUT LOSS . . .

I. PURPOSE:

To increase awareness of available, free (or almost free) leisure opportunities.

To identify 5 inexpensive leisure activities that will be integrated into your lifestyle.

II. GENERAL COMMENTS:

A balance of work, **leisure**, and self-care is a requirement for wellness. However, leisure activities are often excluded from one's life due to financial stress. There is an unlimited number of opportunities available that do not cost anything (or cost very little).

III. POSSIBLE ACTIVITIES:

A. 1. Explain concept of balancing work, **leisure**, and self-care.

2. Facilitate brainstorming on the chalkboard regarding free or almost free leisure opportunities.

3. Encourage group members to choose 5 from the list that they will pursue and write them on their handouts.

4. Ask each group member in turn to describe how he/she will incorporate these into his/her lifestyle.

5. Process benefits of leisure awareness.

B. 1. Write 20-40 free or almost free leisure activities on separate index cards. Shuffle.

2. Instruct each group member to choose 2-3 cards (depending on total number of group members and cards).

3. Ask each member to take a turn and pantomime one of the chosen cards (leisure activities), with the others guessing what it is.

4. Suggest that group members write interesting ones on their handouts as they arise.

5. Conclude with a discussion focused on those written.

6. Process benefits of leisure awareness.

WHAT MOTIVATES ME?

Rank: #1 = most motivating to #12 = least motivating

_____ enjoyment/fun
_____ family and/or friendships
_____ independence/freedom
_____ possessions
_____ mental health
_____ money/savings

_____ personal achievements
_____ physical health/fitness
_____ power/authority/strength
_____ school/career achievements
_____ security/safety
_____ popularity/status

Who can you tell that your #1 is a high-ranking motivator? _____

What benefit might you derive? _____

Who can you tell that your #2 is a high-ranking motivator? _____

What benefit might you derive? _____

Who can you tell that your #11 is a low-ranking motivator? _____

What benefit might you derive? _____

Who can you tell that your #12 is a low-ranking motivator? _____

What benefit might you derive? _____

Motivators

I. PURPOSE:

To develop an understanding of one's personal motivation by ranking the 12 motivators listed.

To recognize with which significant people this information might be shared to increase performance and satisfaction.

II. GENERAL COMMENTS:

Knowing what our motivators are and being able to express them may increase performance and satisfaction. (*As a facilitator, it is important to know what motivates our clients so we can be more therapeutic.*)

III. POSSIBLE ACTIVITIES:

A. 1. Prepare 12 slips of paper with 1 motivator written on each. Put them in a "hat."

    2. Encourage group members to choose one and describe the importance of their motivator to the group.

    3. Instruct group members to complete the handout as indicated.

    4. Process importance of this information.

B. 1. Instruct group members to complete the handout individually.

    2. Encourage members to create a magazine picture collage separated into two sections. On the right side of the paper, place pictures, words, and/or symbols representing high motivators. On the left, low motivators.

    3. Facilitate discussion of personal motivators by asking the following questions:

        a. What do the "pictures" represent?

        b. Why did you place them on that side of the paper?

        c. What people in your life know that these are high or low motivators?

    4. Process importance of this information.

REINFORCERS

(rē·in·fôrs′ers) Things or ways to strengthen yourself to accomplish a desired task.

LIST 5 DESIRED TASKS, EXTERNAL REINFORCERS AND INTERNAL REINFORCERS.

DESIRED TASK	EXTERNAL REINFORCERS	INTERNAL REINFORCERS
I will stop smoking.	I will buy myself a ''treat'' after one day.	I will feel and be healthier.
	I will reward myself by going to a	I won't worry about future diseases.
	movie after one week.	I'll be less offensive to others.
		I'll get attention from others.
		I'll save money.
1		
2		
3		
4		
5		

REINFORCERS

I. PURPOSE:

To increase knowledge of external and internal reinforcers.

To commit to completing a desired task by creating external reinforcers and recognizing internal ones.

II. GENERAL COMMENTS:

It is important to recognize **external reinforcers** as "outside influences" that one can implement to achieve a desired task, and **internal reinforcers** as "natural influences" that result as the desired task is achieved.

III. POSSIBLE ACTIVITIES:

A. 1. Explain concept of external/internal reinforcers using example provided.

2. Encourage group members to fill in 5 desired tasks and their external and internal reinforcers.

3. Facilitate discussion using members' examples.

4. Process meaning of external and internal reinforcers and their importance.

B. 1. Explain concept of external/internal reinforcers using example provided.

2. Encourage group members to fill in 5 desired tasks and their external and internal reinforcers.

3. Collect handouts from all group members.

4. Read one example from each handout encouraging members to guess the author and to elicit feedback.

5. Process meaning of external and internal reinforcers and their importance.

your eating habits

CHECK ALL APPROPRIATE BOXES:

■ ON AN EVERYDAY BASIS...

1. ☐ I eat one "fresh" fruit and one "fresh" vegetable.
2. ☐ For my age, height, body frame, and activity level, I have learned what my appropriate daily needs are to maintain or change my weight.
3. ☐ I control my calorie intake.
4. ☐ I am aware of and limit my cholesterol and fat intake.
5. ☐ I am aware of the possible effects of sugar and limit my sugar intake.
6. ☐ I am aware of my fiber intake.
7. ☐ I am aware of my calcium intake.
8. ☐ I regulate my caffeine intake.
9. ☐ I eat at least three times each day.
10. ☐ I eat slowly in relaxed, appropriate surroundings.
11. ☐ I concentrate on eating during mealtime and do not allow myself to become distracted.
12. ☐ My meals and table arrangements are carefully and thoughtfully planned in advance.
13. ☐ I drink at least eight 8-ounce glasses of water.

■ WITHIN THIS PAST WEEK...

14. ☐ I ate baked or broiled fish.
15. ☐ I ate oatmeal or stone-ground whole-grained bread or crackers.
16. ☐ I have tried 1 "new food" — (a food I never ate before).
17. ☐ I ate at a fast food restaurant no more than 1 time.

SCORE:

14-17 ✓'s — Wow for wellness!!! Wonderful!!!

8-13 ✓'s — Good, with a need for some improvement.

4- 7 ✓'s — OK...however, your work's cut out for you!

0- 3 ✓'s — Uh oh! Take care of yourself soon!

✔ your eating habits

I. PURPOSE:

To take inventory of present eating habits identifying areas for possible improvement.

To increase knowledge of nutrition.

II. GENERAL COMMENTS:

Many factors influence wellness . . . positive eating habits are among them. Those listed in the handout provide a framework for education.

III. POSSIBLE ACTIVITIES:

A. 1. Encourage each group member to complete the handout and score it.

   2. Facilitate discussion with the group noting areas checked and areas for improvement.

   3. Process benefits of positive eating habits.

B. 1. Divide group into small subgroups and work on each question, i.e.:

      7. I regulate my caffeine intake.
         How?
         Why?
         When?

     14. I have tried one "new food."
         What?
         Where?
         Why?
         New ideas?

   2. Invite the dietitian to join the group and educate on principles covered in the handout.

   3. Process benefits of positive eating habits.

ECONOMICAL & HEALTHY EATING includes...

 &

Learning

- ❀ what are vitamin and mineral enriched foods.
- ❀ where you can buy the least expensive and freshest foods.
- ❀ what are the least expensive vitamin/mineral enriched foods.
- ❀ which coupons to cut out and where to find them.
- ❀ what your family will <u>actually</u> eat!
- ❀ which foods are high or low in salt, oil, fiber, sugar.
- ❀ how to read and use labels (grades, ingredients, brands, etc.)
- ❀ the ABC's of meat buying.
- ❀ which "sale" items really benefit you.

Planning

- ❀ to prepare well-balanced adequate meals.
- ❀ to provide nutritious snacks.
- ❀ to store foods properly.
- ❀ to read labels and directions.
- ❀ to eat at home.
- ❀ to bring coupons with you.
- ❀ to buy by the calendar.
- ❀ to cook in a relaxed atmosphere and a safe, comfortable environment.

NOTES: _____

_____

_____

_____

_____

ECONOMICAL & HEALTHY
EATING

I. PURPOSE:

To increase awareness and knowledge of economical and healthy eating habits.

II. GENERAL COMMENTS:

An active approach is needed for "today's eater" - learning and planning. (Appropriate resources might be offered to supplement information in the learning category.)

III. POSSIBLE ACTIVITIES:

A. 1. Review the "learning" components, discussing and sharing practical information.

2. Review the "planning" components using a "how-to" approach.

3. Process the group by asking members to contribute one fact they remember and how it applies to them.

B. 1. Divide the group into 2 teams.

2. Prepare two sets of cards, one for learning and one for planning. Each card will have one of the statements listed from its respective category.

3. Encourage team #1 to take a turn by selecting one card from either set, discuss the concept among themselves and provide an answer or explanation to the whole group.

4. Score as follows:

   2 points - thorough, accurate answer
   1 point - somewhat accurate and thorough
   0 points - incorrect or no answer

   Facilitator will answer and provide input as necessary.

5. Continue the activity (by alternating teams) until all cards are discussed.

6. Allow the "winning" team to choose when to have cooking group to emphasize learned material.

FOOD FOR THOUGHT

At times, we eat in response to our emotions. . . . .

This association between eating and emotions may not interfere with healthy daily living, but at times it can lead to unhealthy behaviors.

It may result in:

- Overeating
- Undereating
- Not eating
- Making poor food choices
- Eating too quickly
- Purging after eating
- _____
- _____

Some of these behaviors can actually indicate or result in serious eating problems, requiring medical attention.

IT IS IMPORTANT TO RECOGNIZE WHEN YOUR EMOTIONS AFFECT YOUR EATING BEHAVIORS!

☑ one of the top bubbles, and then complete the rest of the cartoon.

☐ HMMMM. . . IT'S MEAL TIME. WHY DON'T I FEEL LIKE EATING?

☐ HMMMM. . . I'M NOT REALLY HUNGRY RIGHT NOW. WHY DO I FEEL LIKE EATING?

MAYBE MAYBE I FEEL... BECAUSE I FEEL...

IF I EAT THIS, HOW WILL I FEEL IN AN HOUR? _____

HOW ELSE CAN I COPE WITH THESE FEELINGS? _____

Try to put things in perspective.

Remember . . . we don't sleep every time we feel tired. Similarly, we don't need to eat, or not eat, every time we feel certain emotions.

Do you respond to emotions through food?

Consider the following recommendations:

- Recognize and allow yourself to feel your emotions, reminding yourself that these emotions won't last forever.
- Communicate your feelings openly and honestly with yourself and others.
- Look for alternative activities.
- Use positive self-talk.
- Relax, using methods you have found beneficial in the past.
- Use self-questioning methods — "Why am I eating this food?" "Why am I eating now?" "Why am I not eating at all?"
- Ask for help to create your own healthy food plan.
- _____
- _____
- If your eating behaviors are out of control. . .
  - Seek medical assistance and counseling.
  - Involve your family and/or friends to help.

FOOD FOR THOUGHT

I. PURPOSE:
   To recognize the relationship between eating and emotions. To identify the effect that emotions can have on eating behaviors, which can ultimately affect physical and emotional health.

II. GENERAL COMMENTS:
   Eating or not eating can be a response to certain emotions. These emotions may be triggered by music, people, events, places, holidays, and thoughts about oneself or one's experiences, just to name a few. Physical and emotional well-being can be significantly affected.

III. POSSIBLE ACTIVITIES: This handout can be used in conjunction with EMOTIONS (page 7).

   A. 1. Distribute one blank piece of typing paper to each group member.
       2. Allowing only 3-4 minutes, instruct the group members to create something using the piece of paper, other than using it to write or draw on. Some possibilities might be: a hat, an airplane, gift wrap, a bookmark, etc.
       3. Ask the group to share their responses.
       4. Introduce emotion identification and ask the group to list several emotions on the chalkboard.
       5. Ask the group members to discuss how emotions can/cannot manifest themselves.
       6. Instruct the group to make a comparison between the introductory activity and emotions. Focus the discussion on the concept that one traditional way of using paper is for writing or drawing. One traditional way of responding to emotions is eating or not eating. Just as the group can be creative and resourceful in using a piece of paper, they will be challenged to examine and develop new ways to cope with emotions other than eating or not eating.
       7. Distribute handout and ask the group if they are aware of any emotions that are most likely to trigger an eating response, e.g., angry, anxious, bored, depressed, exhausted, happy, lonely, etc.
       8. Draw attention to the box on the left side of the handout. Discuss different ways that individuals choose to cope with their emotions by using or not using food. Additional possible responses might be: hiding food, secret eating, eating at times other than mealtime, eating in inappropriate places.
       9. Discuss the question "Why do we use food as a coping skill?" Possible responses might be: it's socially acceptable; we need food in order to live; we need to eat at least three times a day; it's easily accessible; it's legal; it's warm, comforting, filling, tasty, gratifying, satisfying, etc.; it's a behavior, due to cultural or ethnic background, that's taught and accepted by my family; eating food can be a reward, or the denial of food can be a punishment; it's a distraction.
      10. Draw attention to the recommendations box on the right side. Discuss the recommendations and ask for any additions.
      11. Instruct the group to complete the cartoon in the center of the handout using their own eating response to emotions.
      12. Ask the group to share their responses as able, eliciting feedback.
      13. Close by asking the group to summarize the activity. Allow each group member to answer the following statement: "Next time I'm coping with my emotions by eating/not eating, I can choose to _____ instead."

   B. 1. Follow steps 1-10 from Activity A.
       2. Focusing attention to the cartoon on the handout, note the two possible eating behaviors in response to emotions.
       3. Divide the group into two subgroups.
       4. Assign one subgroup the role of top left bubble and the other subgroup the top right.
       5. Instruct each subgroup to complete the cartoon according to their assigned role.
       6. Allow 5-6 minutes for this activity.
       7. Reconvene and ask one representative from each subgroup to share their group's responses, eliciting feedback from the others.
       8. Ask the entire group to summarize the activity.
       9. For further discussion, present the question: "How do emotions affect: speed of eating; food choices; where the food is eaten; when the food is most likely to be consumed; how food is eaten, e.g., while standing, out of a paper bag, a styrofoam container, etc.?"
      10. Close by asking each group member to answer the following statement: "Next time I'm coping with my emotions by eating/not eating, I can choose to _____ instead."

OPENING DOORS TO ACHIEVEMENT

Don't allow obstacles to prevent achievements.
Confront these obstacles by doing the following:

FILL IN POSSIBLE ACHIEVEMENTS   **FILL IN POSSIBLE OBSTACLES**   **KEYS TO "UNLOCKING" THESE OBSTACLES**

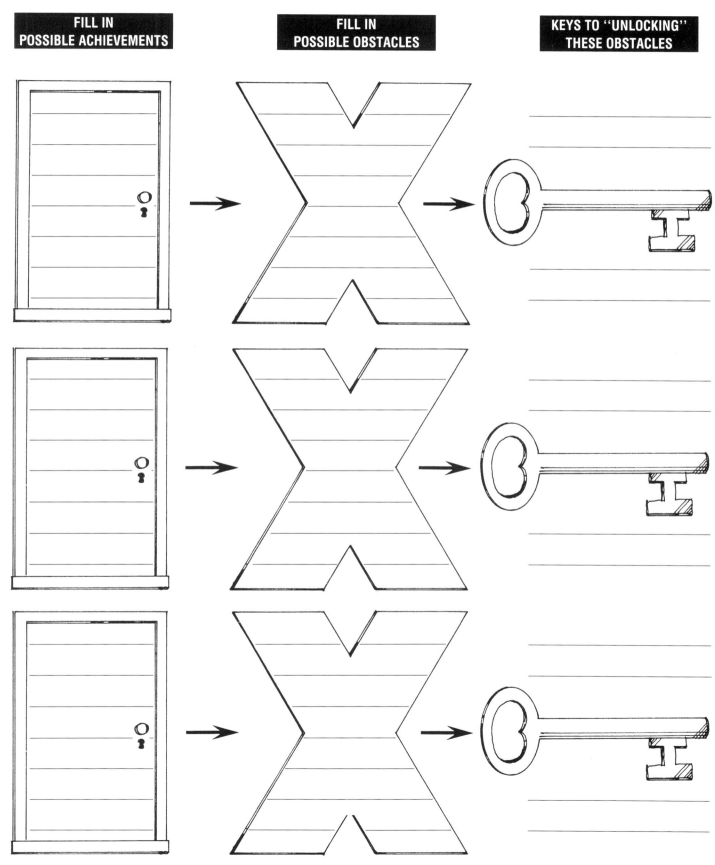

OPENING DOORS TO ACHIEVEMENT

I. PURPOSE:

To increase problem-solving skills by gathering knowledge and experience in confronting obstacles.

II. GENERAL COMMENTS:

"Achieving" increases self-esteem. When one experiences difficulty in achieving, it is vital to recognize what may be preventing the achievement (obstacles) and the ways to remove/alter them (keys).

III. POSSIBLE ACTIVITIES:

A. 1. Use the following example to explain the handout:

- getting
  a
  job

- I'm too old/young.
- I don't have a resume.
- I get nervous when I interview.

- positive self-talk, e.g., "Other people my age have jobs!"
- I'll go to a typesetter.
- I will practice interviews with my . . .

2. Encourage each group member to complete handout.

3. Process impact that problem solving has on self-esteem and goal attainment.

B. 1. Write hypothetical "possible achievements" on separate strips of paper and place in "hat."

2. Divide group into subgroups of 2-3 members.

3. Instruct each subgroup to take one "possible achievement" from "hat" and as a group, problem solve with suggested technique from handout.

4. Facilitate discussion with entire group and encourage subgroups to share their example!

Positive Problem Solving Let's Brainstorm!

I. Identify the problem: (specific) _____

II. Be creative and list options and possible solutions.

☐ _____   ☐ _____
☐ _____   ☐ _____
☐ _____   ☐ _____
☐ _____   ☐ _____
☐ _____   ☐ _____
☐ _____   ☐ _____
☐ _____   ☐ _____
☐ _____   ☐ _____
☐ _____   ☐ _____
☐ _____   ☐ _____

III. ✔ the boxes for those that sound reasonable to you.

IV. Write in the three "best" and why you chose them.

1 _____

_____

2 _____

_____

3 _____

_____

V. Review steps I, II, III, and IV once again and now decide on your plan.

_____

_____

_____

Positive Problem Solving

I. **PURPOSE:**

To increase knowledge and gain experience in the problem-solving technique called "brainstorming."

II. **GENERAL COMMENTS:**

Often when confronted with a problem, it's difficult to see the alternative solutions, options, and possibilities. This technique affords creativity, increases choices, and improves the chances of decision satisfaction.

III. **POSSIBLE ACTIVITIES:**

A. 1. Identify one specific problem on the chalkboard pertaining to all group members, e.g., I watch too much TV or I need more money, and present sections II, III, IV & V.

2. Encourage group members to complete handout individually.

3. Facilitate discussion of I, II, and III.

4. Process possible strengths of this technique.

B. 1. Instruct group members to complete handout using one of their own specific problems.

2. Divide group into subgroups of three to receive feedback from other two people on the completion of exercise.

3. Facilitate discussion with entire group as each member shares their problem and chosen plan.

4. Process importance of looking at all possible options before deciding on a plan to increase decision satisfaction. Discuss the idea that not all chosen plans will necessarily be the "right" ones, but may be the "best" ones at that time. Modifications may need to be made in the future.

DECISION MAKING

You have the right to make decisions that involve challenges, opportunities, and risks.

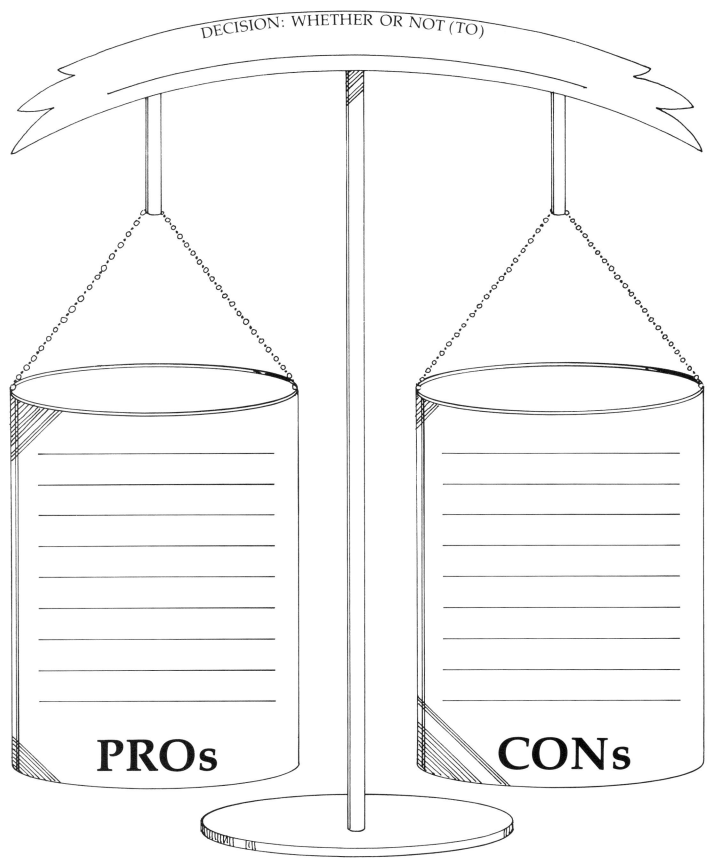

DECISION: WHETHER OR NOT (TO)

PROs

CONs

DECISION MAKING

I. PURPOSE:

To increase decision-making skills by learning and experiencing the method of "weighing things out."

II. GENERAL COMMENTS:

It is easy to get overwhelmed with information when making a difficult decision. Internal conflict may arise when choosing the **best** option for yourself.

III. POSSIBLE ACTIVITIES:

A. 1. Instruct group members to fill in a difficult decision to make in the DECISION: WHETHER OR NOT (TO) space.

2. Encourage them to "weigh things out" by filling in the pro's and con's and then by taking a look at both sides of the issue.

3. Process the benefits of using this decision-making method.

B. 1. Encourage group members to brainstorm decisions people often face, on the chalkboard.

2. Choose one and use the method of "weighing things out" with the group.

3. Elicit feedback regarding this decision-making method.

4. Give homework assignment to complete the handout as described. Write the decisions on the back. Hand in to group leader next session. At that session, collect completed handouts. Read the front aloud and encourage group members to guess what the writer decided.

5. Process the benefits of using this decision-making method.

What's the worst
thing that can
happen if I try?

_____

If I never try,
I'll never know if
I can do it!

If I risk nothing,
I risk . . .

_____

What have
I got to lose?

_____

Why not?

Why not
me?

Why not
now?

Say
"I can do it!"

Risk: _____

So, what's
stopping me?

_____

**"GOPHER"
IT!**

What's
my risk?

_____

Say . . .
"I
WILL
DO
IT!"

START

FINISH!

Plan: _____

"GOPHER" IT!

I. PURPOSE:

To promote risk taking.

II. GENERAL COMMENTS:

The "go-for-it" pathway offers helpful questions and reminders inspiring a risk-taking attitude.

III. POSSIBLE ACTIVITIES:

A. 1. Read the handout aloud to the group, beginning at "start" and completing at "finish."

2. Facilitate brainstorming of hypothetical risks and discuss each step from start to finish.

3. Process values of risk taking.

B. 1. Instruct group members to choose one risk they face and write it under the gopher.

2. Encourage members to write possible responses along the horseshoe and then include a plan or goal on the bottom of the page.

3. Facilitate discussion as individuals share their plan or goal.

4. Process values of risk taking.

To Risk or Not to Risk ???.....

..... Risk taking allows the opportunity for growth, change, and experience.....

..... Remember that to risk nothing in life is to risk everything.....

..... Self-esteem enhancement relies on challenging oneself to grow.....
therefore, to risk.....

..... Life is full of risks ready to be taken.....choices ready to be noticed.....
and skills ready to be strengthened.....

..... Which path will you follow?.....

I have the opportunity to:

1. *take courses for education or special interest* _____

2. _____

3. _____

	If I choose To Risk, then...		If I choose Not To Risk, then...	
	I may gain:	**I may lose:**	**I may gain:**	**I may lose:**
1.	credits experience self-confidence new friends	time leisure friendships tuition sleep	time increased leisure no added stress security stability	adventure new experiences accomplishment
2.				
3.				

To Risk or Not to Risk ???.....

I. PURPOSE:

To promote decision making by evaluating risks to take and risks to decline.

II. GENERAL COMMENTS:

In every risk, there is something to gain and to lose. If no risk is taken, there is also something to gain and to lose.

III. POSSIBLE ACTIVITIES:

A. 1. Explain with the following examples:

I have the opportunity to	If I risk		If I don't risk	
	I may gain	I may lose	I may gain	I may lose
Start a business	1. money 2. prestige 3. self-confidence 4. autonomy 5. experience	1. money 2. time	1. sense of stability 2. time	1. sense of adventure 2. opportunity for greater job satisfaction 3. respect for myself 4. creativity

2. Encourage group members to contribute hypothetical or possible risks and write them on separate strips of paper. Put in "hat."

3. Instruct group members to choose one from the "hat." Each member takes a turn and reads his/hers, offering input for each column of the handout.

4. Process benefits of handout by eliciting feedback from group members.

B. 1. Instruct each group member to complete handout with personal situations.

2. Collect and read each one aloud.

3. Instruct group members to guess the author of each and offer feedback.

4. Process benefits of handout by eliciting feedback from group members.

SHOOT FOR THE STARS!

I. PURPOSE:

To set expectations which promote risk taking.

II. GENERAL COMMENTS:

Although goals need to be realistic and attainable, it is important to ''set sights'' high to ensure personal growth.

III. POSSIBLE ACTIVITIES:

A. 1. Encourage group members to write 3 possible expectations, risks, beliefs and/or hopes.

2. Facilitate discussion using group members' examples.

3. Process importance of self-growth and risk taking.

B. 1. Encourage group members to write 3 possible expectations, risks, beliefs, and/or hopes.

2. Collect handouts and read each aloud.

3. Encourage others to guess the author.

4. Process importance of self-growth and risk taking.

What's in a Name?

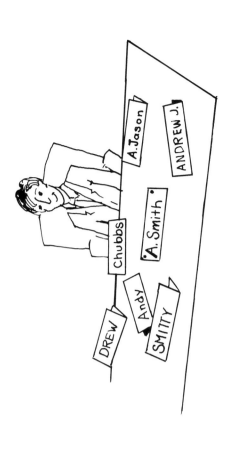

All my names: (past/present) [first, middle, last, nicknames]	Who calls or called me that?	What is or was my role?	How do I feel thinking about it now?

What's in a Name?

I. **PURPOSE:**

To increase awareness of present roles and role satisfaction.

To reminisce regarding past roles and role satisfaction via names we are known by presently, or we have been known by in the past.

II. **GENERAL COMMENTS:**

Many people have a collection of names they've been known by throughout their lives. Often, these names are associated with roles or relationships.

III. **POSSIBLE ACTIVITIES:**

A. 1. Instruct group members to complete handout horizontally encouraging participants to recall all names.

   2. Choose one role, (e.g., friend, parent, or child) and facilitate discussion with group members that identified a name associated with that role. Continue choosing roles until all are shared.

   3. Process benefits of reminiscing and acknowledging roles and role satisfaction.

B. 1. Instruct group members to complete handout horizontally encouraging participants to recall all names.

   2. Collect all handouts and read aloud one at a time, encouraging group members to guess the author and discuss insights as they arise.

   3. Process benefits of reminiscing and acknowledging roles and role satisfaction.

ROLES

My roles:

1. _____

2. _____

3. _____

4. _____

5. _____

Choose one role: _____

Things I do well within this role. **FOCUS ON POSITIVES!**	Things I don't do well within this role. **ROOM FOR CHANGE!**
1.	
2.	
3.	
4.	
5.	

❧ ROLES ❧

I. PURPOSE:

To acknowledge one's present roles in life.

To focus on what one does well within these roles.

To recognize areas of improvement within these roles promoting role satisfaction.

II. GENERAL COMMENTS:

A role can be defined as a position that one holds in life which constitutes a portion of his/her self-image. Identity and satisfaction lie within how one feels within these roles. Attempts can be made to improve role satisfaction.

III. POSSIBLE ACTIVITIES:

A. 1. Prepare a game by cutting up slips of paper and writing hypothetical roles on each, e.g., sister/brother, father/mother, worker/student/volunteer, friend.

2. Game proceeds as follows:

a. one group member chooses a paper from the "hat" and describes things he/she does well within that role and things that he/she does not do well within that role.

b. if role does not apply to him/her presently, ask the individual if he/she would like to have this role. The group member can then discuss what positive attributes he/she would bring to this role and areas he/she would need to work on.

c. if he/she does not wish to address the one chosen, the group member may choose another role from the "hat."

d. game continues with each group member having a turn.

3. Process need for role satisfaction.

B. 1. Encourage group members to complete the handout and give to the facilitator.

2. Read from the handouts and encourage others to guess the author.

3. Process need for role satisfaction.

● My birth date _____

MY LIFE: past – present – future

● My death at age _____

MY LIFE: past – present – future

I.   **PURPOSE:**

To increase self-awareness by reminiscing about past life events, reporting on present life situations, and foreseeing future life plans.

II. **GENERAL COMMENTS:**

Developing a "Life Line" can help put events in perspective, provide a general outlook on life, and suggest a sense of future.

III. **POSSIBLE ACTIVITIES:**

A. 1. Instruct group members to complete developmental life line with significant life events, starting from birthdate on the left to age of death on the right. Depictions can be words, symbols, or drawings.

   2. Facilitate discussion by sharing completed projects.

   3. Process importance of acknowledging past, present, future.

B. 1. Distribute strips of paper to each individual.

   2. Encourage group members to write each significant life event on one side of the paper and classify it on the other as past, present, or future. Instruct them to divide their papers into three piles.

   3. Collect from group members, and combine all the "pasts," "presents," and "futures," into three piles.

   4. Instruct group members to choose one piece of paper from one of the three piles and read it aloud. The person to whom it belongs shares details/insights regarding that event.

   5. Proceed until all have had a chance to share at least one.

   6. Process importance of acknowledging past, present, future.

Be your own best friend

"Sometimes the best thing you can do for yourself is reflect..."

- When was the last time I truly felt good about myself? _____

  _____

- What were the circumstances?

  work/school _____

  approximate age _____

  lifestyle _____

  financial situation _____

  relationships _____

  self-image _____

  health _____

  my behavior _____

  roles _____

- How can I realistically restore any of these circumstances? _____

  _____

- Therefore, my goal(s) is/are ... _____

  _____

Be your own best friend

I. PURPOSE:

To increase self-awareness by reflecting on positive past experiences.

To identify ways to restore those circumstances or create similar ones.

II. GENERAL COMMENTS:

In times of increased stress and/or depression, it may be difficult to remember when life was "better." It can be valuable to reflect on satisfying times to identify and begin to restore some of the surrounding circumstances.

III. POSSIBLE ACTIVITIES: This handout can be used in conjuction with GOAL SETTING PRACTICE SHEET (page 13).

A. 1. Encourage group members to complete handout.

2. Instruct each individual to read his/her responses aloud to the group.

3. Discuss importance of setting goals to make positive changes in your life, as well as recognizing that change **is** possible.

B. 1. Discuss concept of "being your own best friend."

2. Encourage group members to complete handout thoroughly.

3. Collect all handouts and shuffle.

4. Distribute them so that each group member has one (not their own).

5. Give each individual an opportunity to read aloud the handout he/she was given and then guess the author.

6. If guess is incorrect, actual person then identifies self and restates "goal."

7. Continue until all members have had a turn.

8. Discuss importance of setting goals to make positive changes in your life, as well as recognizing that change IS possible.

Influential people who have made an *imprint* on my life!

	Influential people in my life.	What about them influenced/influences me?	How did/or does that influence my behavior?
FAMILY MEMBERS			
FRIENDS			
TEACHERS			
PUBLIC FIGURES			
FICTIONAL CHARACTERS			
LOVES			
PEOPLE IN HISTORY			
CELEBRITIES			
CLERGY			
OTHER			

Influential people who have made an *imprint* on my life!

I. PURPOSE:

To increase self-awareness by recognizing how people have influenced one's life.

II. GENERAL COMMENTS:

Many factors influence who we are today, e.g., education, money, values, religion, jobs, and **people**. This handout encourages one to look at the positive and/or negative influences people have had on his/her life.

III. POSSIBLE ACTIVITIES:

A. 1. Use the examples below to explain activity.

    2. Encourage group members to complete handout.

    3. Facilitate discussion.

    4. Process feelings experienced as a result of doing this activity.

	Influential people...	What about them...	How did/or...
Fictional characters	Wicked Witch of the West	she was evil and intentionally hurt people	allows me to be more sensitive to my children's fears
Family	Grandfather	taking me to the circus	I love the circus and the memories it brings.

B. 1. Write several examples of each category on separate index cards:

    a. FAMILY MEMBERS (father, sister, aunt, grandfather)

    b. PEOPLE IN HISTORY (J.F.K., Jonas Salk, Harriet Beecher Stowe)

    2. Instruct a group member to choose one.

    3. If this person has had an "imprint" on his/her life, he/she can share "what about them influenced me" and "how did or does that influence my behavior." If this person had no "imprint," the individual can pass the card to the right until someone can contribute or until the card goes back to the beginning. Encourage the next group member to choose a new card, and the game continues.

    4. Process feelings experienced as a result of doing this activity.

Affirmations . . . which help me to be

an A+ me!

PROGRESS

PHYSICAL STATUS

1. I _____

2. I _____

SOCIAL STATUS

1. I _____

2. I _____

INTELLECTUAL STATUS

1. I _____

2. I _____

PROGRESS

EMOTIONAL STATUS

1. I _____

2. I _____

SPIRITUAL STATUS

1. I _____

2. I _____

Grade ___A+___

Promoted to: _School of Positive Thinking._

Comments: _This promotion will last as long as you maintain this A+ attitude!_

_____
(Signature)

Affirmations... which help me to be

an $A+$ me!

I. PURPOSE:

To increase self-esteem by making positive affirmations.

II. GENERAL COMMENTS:

Positive affirmations are self-esteem boosters!! There are several ways to state affirmations. Here is a list of some of them:

A. I am . . .

B. I can . . .

C. I accept . . .

D. I have . . .

E. I feel . . .

III. POSSIBLE ACTIVITIES:

A. 1. Use the following examples (or your own) to illustrate the concept of the handout:

a. PHYSICAL STATUS - I am physically fit.

b. SOCIAL STATUS - I have three very close friends who support me.

c. INTELLECTUAL STATUS - I can learn to manage my money better by taking an adult education class at a junior college.

d. EMOTIONAL STATUS - I feel relaxed and in control of my life.

e. SPIRITUAL STATUS - I accept myself and others unconditionally.

2. Instruct group members to complete handout.

3. Encourage each member to share his/her complete list of affirmations.

4. Process importance of positive self-talk in regard to self-esteem.

B. 1. Brainstorm with group members possible items to include within each category of handout.

2. Instruct group members to complete handout.

3. Prepare card game by labeling four index cards for each category listed in A.1. Place in a "hat" and shuffle the twenty cards.

4. Ask each group member to choose a card and identify his/her affirmations within that category.

5. Continue until all have shared and all cards have been discussed.

6. Process importance of positive self-talk in regard to self-esteem.

I *will* like myself **A** to **Z** !

A. _____

B. _____

C. _____

D. _____

E. _____

F. _____

G. _____

h. _____

i. _____

J. _____

K. _____

L. _____

m. _____

n. _____

o. _____

p. _____

Q. _____

R. _____

S. _____

t. _____

U. _____

V. _____

W. _____

X. _exceptional_____

y. _____

Z. _____

I. **PURPOSE:**

To increase self-esteem by acknowledging and accepting positive qualities regarding oneself.

II. **GENERAL COMMENTS:**

Positive affirmations can be created by using the alphabet as an outline. Acknowledging one's own positive qualities can be a powerful tool in boosting self-esteem.

III. **POSSIBLE ACTIVITIES:**

A. 1. Instruct each group member to complete handout using the following format: ''I will like myself because I am . . .''

    2. After each letter, a phrase or word beginning with that letter (or sound, if you like) should follow to complete the sentence, e.g.:
       R - receptive to new ideas
       X - exceptional in drawing cartoons

    3. Process benefits of positive affirmations and impact on self-esteem.

B. 1. Distribute the handouts and ask each group member to put his/her name at the top of the page.

    2 Collect and redistribute handouts so that everyone has someone else's paper.

    3. Instruct members to insert one adjective or phrase after one letter of the alphabet, describing something positive about that individual.

    4. Encourage each group member to put one positive comment on each of his peers' handouts, continuing to pass them around until 26 comments are on each and all are returned.

    5. Invite each member to read his/her handout aloud to group.

    6. Process benefits of positive affirmations and impact on self-esteem.

Certificate

In recognition of your efforts and accomplishments in the following area(s):

_____

_____

_____

(name)

is awarded this certificate at _____

(facility)

Stay well!

_____

(date)

Certificate

I. **PURPOSE:**

To increase self-esteem by recognizing efforts and accomplishments.

II. **GENERAL COMMENTS:**

It is easy to allow noteworthy efforts and accomplishments to go unrecognized. With this handout these events can be written and displayed to serve as a visual reminder of success.

III. **POSSIBLE ACTIVITIES:**

A. Complete this handout to recognize . . .

1. Completion of a class, lecture, hospital stay, other activity.

2. Increased skill level (assertion, time management, stress management).

3. Attendance.

4. Other noteworthy efforts and accomplishments.

B. 1. Ask one member in the group to temporarily leave the room.

2. While he/she is out, ask the other members to decide which positive areas to recognize in the individual at that particular time.

3. Encourage one member to complete the certificate and all participants sign.

4. Allow member to rejoin group, be presented the certificate, receive standing ovation and applause.

5. Proceed with all members.

6. Process benefits of this activity.

Self-Esteem

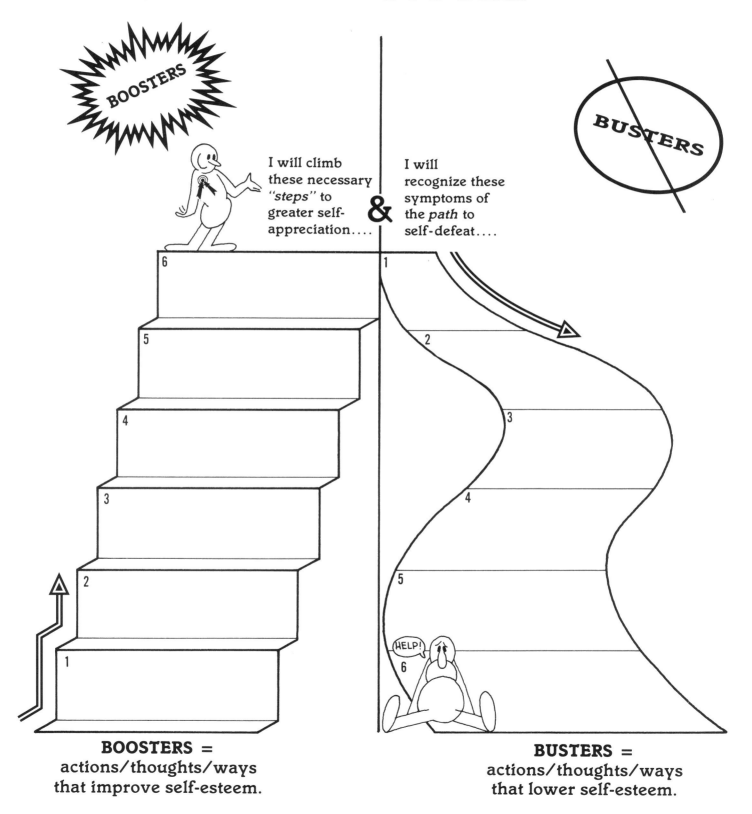

BOOSTERS

BUSTERS

I will climb these necessary "steps" to greater self-appreciation....

&

I will recognize these symptoms of the path to self-defeat....

HELP!

BOOSTERS =
actions/thoughts/ways
that improve self-esteem.

BUSTERS =
actions/thoughts/ways
that lower self-esteem.

Self-Esteem

I. PURPOSE:

To increase self-esteem by creating *steps* to greater self-appreciation and recognizing symptoms of self-defeat.

II. GENERAL COMMENTS:

Self-esteem boosters are positive *steps* one can take to lead to greater self-appreciation. Self-esteem busters are negative influences that lead to self-defeat.

III. POSSIBLE ACTIVITIES:

   A. 1. Explain concept by giving examples:

       self-esteem boosters - taking a continuing education class, having my hair done, going out with friends two times a week

       self-esteem busters - calling myself "stupid," not saying "no," being behind in my bills, work, etc.

      2. Instruct group members to complete handouts.

      3. Collect and read each aloud with others guessing the author of each.

      4. Process benefits of this activity.

   B. 1. Facilitate brainstorming on chalkboard regarding ideas for each category.

      2. Encourage discussion regarding impact of self-esteem busters and boosters on wellness.

      3. Process benefits of this activity.

Sleep Well . . . $_z{}^z{}^z{}^z$

When restful sleep is not a consistent part of your lifestyle, check yourself out. These factors can influence your quality of sleep . . .

✔ one or more

☐ use of alcohol   Sleeping environment: ☐ stressors
☐ use of other drugs   ☐ noise level   ☐ fluctuating sleep times
☐ caffeine intake   ☐ temperature   ☐ lack of exercise
☐ new medication   ☐ lighting   ☐ eating habits
☐ illness   ☐ visual surroundings   ☐ Other _____

Now having identified the area(s) that may be affecting your restfulness, make a list of possible ways to counteract each factor.

DESCRIPTION OF INFLUENCING FACTORS:	WHAT I WILL DO TO COUNTERACT THIS:

Sleep Well . . . z^{z z z}

I. PURPOSE:

To increase awareness of factors which may affect quality of sleep.

To identify ways to improve quality of sleep.

II. GENERAL COMMENTS:

Quality of sleep is determined by a combination of factors. It is valuable to evaluate present sleep patterns and habits, and identify a specific plan to counteract negative influences.

III. POSSIBLE ACTIVITIES:

A. 1. Encourage group members to complete handout.

2. Ask members for feedback regarding:
   —checked boxes and any "others"
   —description of influencing factors
   —counteractions

3. Process importance of healthy sleep habits and impact on performance areas.

B. 1. Make a card game by writing healthy and unhealthy sleep habits on separate index cards. Refer to handout SUGGESTIONS FOR SLEEPING SOUNDLY (page 39).

2. Divide group into two teams.

3. Instruct Team #1 representative to choose a card from the pile and read aloud. Team #2 will be given 1 point if they identify the habit correctly as healthy or unhealthy and another point if they can explain why.

4. Encourage teams to take turns until all cards are discussed or time is up.

5. Applaud both teams for their efforts!

Suggestions for Sleeping Soundly

Taking these sleep guidelines into account with your daily routine may bring you a more refreshing morning. . .every morning!

1. _____ at the same time every morning, 7 days a week, regardless of the time you fell asleep or how well you slept throughout the night.

2. Follow a _____ when readying for bed, whether at home or away, e.g., brushing teeth, washing face, taking a warm bath, slow stretching, reading a short magazine article, saying a prayer, etc.

3. Eat a light, _____ snack prior to bed if you have hunger pangs. Milk and tuna fish are known to contain L-tryptophan which helps to induce sleep. Eliminating the hunger itself will allow for improved sleep as well.

4. Avoid _____ and _____ in the evening hours as they will disturb normal sleep pattern.

5. _____ daily in the late afternoon or early evening to allow for deepened sleep during the night.

6. Remain on a daily activity schedule seven days a week, to include work, _____, and self care.

7. Spend a specified time _____ to deal with unresolved issues, new problems/ conflicts, and to plan your next day's activities. Leaving these thoughts for bedtime will only create "_____," decreasing your ability to fall asleep and experience quality sleep.

8. Design your _____ to be a _____ environment to sleep, e.g., reduce lighting, minimize noises and visual distractions, moderate room temperature (approx. 65°F).

9. Do not _____ during the day because it most often reduces quantity and quality of sleep at night. Take breaks to refresh yourself instead.

10. Utilize your bedroom for sleeping and _____ _____ only. By using it for exercising, studying, watching TV, etc., you are giving your brain the message that the room is a place for wakeful activity, even stress.

11. If you are unable to fall asleep after 15-20 minutes in bed, _____ your _____ to another activity in another room until you become sleepy.

12. Consistently using_____ will interfere with sleep, so it is advised to reduce its usage and/or develop a plan to quit.

13. _____ may not be recommended as a component of your normal routine for sleep. Occasional use may be needed with supervision of a doctor, however reduction of use and elimination is often encouraged as soon as possible. Check with your doctor.

14. Engage in a relaxing activity prior to bedtime to help you unwind both _____ and _____.

15. Follow the guidelines in #1-14 for increased sleeping _____!!

Word Choices to Fill-in the Blanks:

alcohol	mind-racing
attention	nap
bedroom	nutritional
caffeine	physically
conducive	routine
daily	sexual activity
divert	sleeping pills
exercise	success
leisure	tobacco
mentally	wake up

Suggestions for Sleeping Soundly

I. PURPOSE:

To increase awareness of good sleeping habits.

To identify areas of change needed to improve quality of sleep.

II. GENERAL COMMENTS:

How one prepares for sleep and feels prior to sleep can influence the quality of rest achieved. There are important tips to keep in mind regarding nutrition, exercise, stress, and environment which can increase restfulness and overall wellness.

III. POSSIBLE ACTIVITIES:

A. 1. Explain concept of quality of sleep in relation to wellness.

2. Instruct group members to compete handout by filling in all blanks using the words provided.

3. When completed, discuss answers.

4. Key is as follows:
   1. wake up
   2. routine
   3. nutritional
   4. alcohol, caffeine
   5. exercise
   6. leisure
   7. daily, mind-racing
   8. bedroom, conducive
   9. nap
   10. sexual activity
   11. divert, attention
   12. tobacco
   13. sleeping pills
   14. physically, mentally
   15. success

5. Process benefits of this activity.

B. 1. Explain concept of quality of sleep in relation to wellness.

2. Instruct group members to compete handout by filling in all blanks using the words provided.

3. When completed, discuss answers.

4. Key is as follows:
   1. wake up
   2. routine
   3. nutritional
   4. alcohol, caffeine
   5. exercise
   6. leisure
   7. daily, mind-racing
   8. bedroom, conducive
   9. nap
   10. sexual activity
   11. divert, attention
   12. tobacco
   13. sleeping pills
   14. physically, mentally
   15. success

5. Process benefits of this activity.

6. Instruct group members to determine how many of the 15 guidelines they *do* follow and how they can increase this number by establishing an action plan.

Are you "under" STRESS?

Name _____

STRESS SYMPTOMS

I know I'm under stress when I...(✓)

☐ Cry more than usual
☐ Can't sleep
☐ Eat more than usual
☐ Am irritable
☐ Resort to the use of alcohol/drugs
☐ Have "physical complaints"

☐ Have difficulty concentrating/focusing
☐ Sleep more than usual
☐ Don't feel like eating
☐ Am on the move all the time—fidgety
☐ Become overly sensitive
☐ Don't feel like doing anything
☐ Other _____

STRESS REDUCERS

When I see these "symptoms," I will...(✓ and be specific)

☐ Go for a walk _____ for _____ mins.
☐ Read a good book _____ for _____ mins.
☐ Go shopping at _____ for _____ mins.
☐ Exercise _____ for _____ mins.
☐ Listen to music on the _____
☐ Watch my favorite T.V. program(s) _____
☐ Use relaxation techniques _____
☐ Take some time for myself by _____
☐ Do something I'm skilled at _____ for _____ mins.
☐ Talk to my friend, therapist, doctor, someone else named _____
☐ Say "No" to _____
☐ Confront the situation by _____
☐ Limit certain behaviors _____
☐ Prioritize my responsibilities # 1 _____
                                    # 2 _____
                                    # 3 _____
☐ Other _____

**Are you
"under"
STRESS?**

I. PURPOSE:

   To increase awareness of stress symptoms and reducers, promoting effective management of stress.

II. GENERAL COMMENTS:

   People are often unaware of their stress symptoms. An active approach to stress management includes recognizing stress symptoms and pairing them with specific stress reducers. In this manner, one can develop new coping skill patterns.

III. POSSIBLE ACTIVITIES:

   A. 1. Explain that stress symptoms "creep up" slowly and often with no "announcement."

   2. Instruct group members to complete handout.

   3. Divide group into subgroups of three to share responses.

   4. After a specified time, encourage group members to reconvene and process the benefits of coping with stress.

   B. 1. Distribute handouts to group members and give them 60 seconds to look at the handout, remembering as much as they can.

   2. After the handouts are turned over, encourage group members to recall as much as they can as someone writes on the chalkboard under two categories: symptoms and coping skills.

   3. Complete the chalkboard list by referring to handout and facilitate discussion encouraging group members to add to list.

   4. Instruct group members to complete handout for homework assignment.

   5. Process benefits of coping with stress.

How I'm Going to be "On Top Of" STRESS !

Name _____

#1 When I see that I _____
Stress Symptom(s)

I will _____

_____

#2 When I see that I _____
Stress Symptom(s)

I will _____

_____

#3 When I see that I _____
Stress Symptom(s)

I will _____

_____

#4 When I see that I _____
Stress Symptom(s)

I will _____

_____

#5 When I see that I _____
Stress Symptom(s)

I will _____

_____

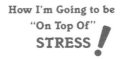

How I'm Going to be "On Top Of" STRESS!

I. PURPOSE:

To improve stress management by use of the self-contract method.

II. GENERAL COMMENTS:

Being able to identify stress symptoms and pair them with specific stress reducers is a powerful way to change behavior and increase self-management.

III. POSSIBLE ACTIVITIES:

A. 1. Elicit possible stress symptoms from group members and list them on the left side of the chalkboard.

2. Do the same with stress reducers on the right side of the chalkboard.

3. Encourage group members to see if any of them could be paired and used as effective self-contracting goals.

4. Instruct group members to complete handout with goals for relieving their own stress symptoms.

5. Process importance of stress management and impact of self-contracts.

B. 1. Use this handout in conjunction with ARE YOU UNDER STRESS? (page 40). Instruct group members to create goals from their checked boxes.

2. Encourage group members to read their completed self-contract for the entire group and seek feedback.

3. Process importance of stress management and impact of self-contracts.

"SUCCESS WITH STRESS"

REPROGRAMMING

Life consistently presents us with changes and these changes create stress. Discovering how we manage life in various situations will allow us to succeed with stress rather than experience *di*stress.

Life Situations	"Out with the Old" PATTERNS	"In with the New" COPING SKILLS
1.		
2.		
3.		
4.		
5.		

REPROGRAMMING IS:

recognizing negative thought PATTERNS which lead to unhealthy behaviors, and then…changing your thinking to allow healthier COPING SKILLS to develop.

"SUCCESS WITH STRESS"

I. PURPOSE:

To improve stress management by changing unhealthy patterns into healthy ones.

II. GENERAL COMMENTS:

Stress management is an active process which contributes to wellness. "Reprogramming" is one technique which may encourage healthy coping skills.

III. POSSIBLE ACTIVITIES:

A. 1. Present top portion of handout.

2. Use the following examples (and your own) to illustrate the idea of "reprogramming":

Life Situation	"Out with the Old"	"In with the New"
My friend calls me and I'm really busy.	I would talk and then get angry at her and myself.	I would assert myself saying "This is not a good time for me to talk ... I'd like to call you back."
My wife lost $50 in the lottery.	I would hit her.	I would tell her that I'm leaving the house for 15-20 minutes to take a walk so I can calm down.

3. Encourage members to complete handout.

4. Process concept of "reprogramming" with reference to definition at bottom of page.

B. 1. Explain concept of "reprogramming" and give directions for handout.

2. Encourage group members to fill in columns 1 and 2 only.

3. Call on each member in sequence to share one life situation and "old" pattern.

4. Encourage rest of group to brainstorm possible "new" coping skills for the situation shared.

5. Suggest the individual choose one option and write it in his/her handout column #3.

6. Continue until all have shared.

7. Process concept of "reprogramming" with reference to definition at bottom of page.

NO ONE is an
"Iₛ-LAND"

- One valuable "SURVIVAL SKILL" is having supports in our lives to help us cope.

- Fill in the names of your "SUPPORTS" above.

- If you were not able to fill in all 5, how or where can you find them?

_____

_____

_____

_____

NO ONE is an

"Is-LAND"

I. PURPOSE:

To identify present support systems and possible need for additional ones.

To identify ways to increase support systems.

II. GENERAL COMMENTS:

It is important to have at least five supports at any given time in one's life. A network including individuals, groups, pets, organizations, family, friends, etc., allows for a more effective means of support.

III. POSSIBLE ACTIVITIES:

A. 1. Encourage group members to brainstorm possible support systems on chalkboard, including financial, emotional, social, spiritual, professional, etc.

2. Ask group members to consider these when completing handout. Explain handout further.

3. Encourage group members to share their identified supports with entire group, seeking feedback regarding how/where to increase number as needed.

4. Process benefits of support systems in regards to wellness.

B. 1. Explain concept of support systems.

2. Encourage group members to complete handout first. Then on separate sheet of paper or back of handout write *why* each of these supports are helpful to them.

3. Give each member an opportunity to share his/her list of supports and why they are helpful.

4. Process by encouraging group members to identify something he/she learned from this activity.

NAME:	TYPE OF SERVICE:	ADDRESS:	PHONE #:
1			
2			
3			
4			
5			

**There
ARE
community resources !**

I. PURPOSE:

To increase awareness of community resources which may act to increase one's support system.

II. GENERAL COMMENTS:

Community resources are available, but often people are unaware of them. By educating individuals about possible community resources and encouraging them to list the most applicable, this handout can then be a visual reminder and assist with follow-through.

III. POSSIBLE ACTIVITIES:

A. 1. Display available pamphlets, booklets, leaflets, brochures, and flyers.

2. Encourage group members to read and choose appropriate community resources for their own use.

3. Facilitate discussion by encouraging each group member to share his/her list during a "good-bye" session prior to "discharge" to assist with the transition.

B. 1. Write 40-50 possible community resources on index cards possibly divided into several categories, e.g., religious, educational, volunteer, emotional support, recreational, etc.

2. For a discharge-planning session, encourage each individual to choose a card from any category, and then read aloud.

3. Instruct group members interested in this resource to write it on their handout.

4. Proceed until all group members have had a turn and five resources are listed on each sheet.

5. Discuss importance of support networks, and process benefits of doing this activity.

Are you on "BRAIN OVERLOAD"?

Do you feel like you have a "*million*" things to get done . . . RIGHT NOW?

1st Step — Write them down

2nd Step — Indicate #1 — if this is the "*best*" use of your time RIGHT NOW.
Indicate #2 — if this is a "*good*" use of your time RIGHT NOW.
Indicate #3 — if this is a "*waste*" of your time RIGHT NOW.

3rd Step — Insert all of your #1's in the "*Today*" list on page 2.
Insert all of your #2's in the "*Next Few Days*" list on page 2.
Insert all of your #3's in the "*Waste of my time right now*!" list on page 2.

A _____ = # _____

B _____ = # _____

C _____ = # _____

D _____ = # _____

E _____ = # _____

F _____ = # _____

G _____ = # _____

H _____ = # _____

I _____ = # _____

J _____ = # _____

(continued on page 2)

Are you on

"BRAIN OVERLOAD"?

I. PURPOSE:

To improve time management skills by prioritizing tasks.

II. GENERAL COMMENTS:

"Brain Overload" refers to the overwhelming feeling that occurs when there are an increasing number of pressures and responsibilites to be addressed. Ineffective time management can be a stressor.

III. POSSIBLE ACTIVITIES:

A. 1. Encourage group members to complete handout as indicated.
Possible examples ....

   a. rearranging drawers = #3

   b. grocery shopping = #1

   c. mowing lawn   = #2

  2. Distribute BRAIN OVERLOAD handout (page 46).
Instruct group members to complete this according to priorities, i.e., today, next few days, waste of my time right now.

  3. Facilitate discussion by asking group members to share their top priorities with others and insights gained from doing this activity.

B. 1. Begin with a discussion regarding the importance of prioritizing to decrease stress/increase success.

  2. Encourage group members to cite:

   (a) times when they allowed tasks to get out of control and create stress.

   (b) times in their lives when effective time management increased their sense of success.

  3. Explain system utilized in handout.

  4. Instruct group members to complete handout as a "homework assignment" and bring to next session.

  5. During next session, process benefit of this activity.

Brain Overload?

#1   **Today**

_____

_____

_____

_____

_____

#2   **Next Few Days**

_____

_____

_____

_____

_____

#3   **Waste of my time right now!**

_____

_____

_____

_____

_____

Brain Overload?

I. PURPOSE:

To improve time management skills by placing tasks into three time slots for completion.

II. GENERAL COMMENTS:

This handout can be used in conjunction with ARE YOU ON BRAIN OVERLOAD? (page 45), or individually as a visual reminder and an organizational tool.

III. POSSIBLE ACTIVITIES:

A. 1. Instruct group members to complete this handout after finishing ARE YOU ON BRAIN OVERLOAD? (page 45).

2. Process resultant feelings of organizing tasks into time slots.

B. 1. Distribute a packet of seven handouts to each group member.

2. Instruct each group member to complete one form every morning to prepare for the day ahead.

3. Collect finished packets after one week.

4. Elicit feedback as to possible benefits of this exercise.

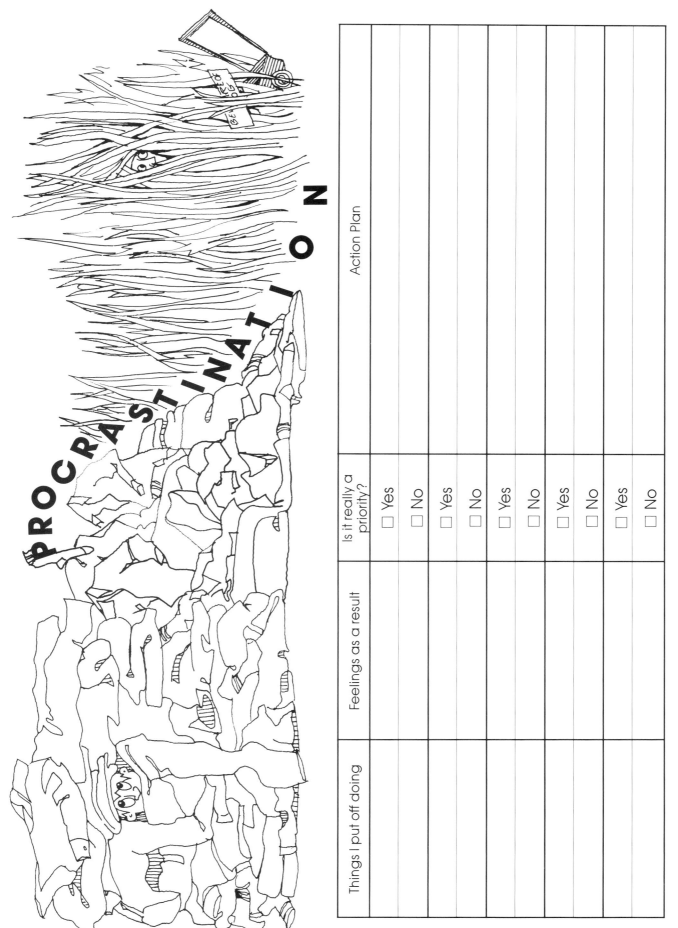

PROCRASTINATION

Things I put off doing	Feelings as a result	Is it really a priority?	Action Plan
		☐ Yes ☐ No	
		☐ Yes ☐ No	
		☐ Yes ☐ No	
		☐ Yes ☐ No	
		☐ Yes ☐ No	

"Time offers us possibilities to create opportunities."

I. PURPOSE:

To improve time management skills.

II. GENERAL COMMENTS:

Procrastination is an ineffective way of managing time. By assessing a task's relative priority, one can use an "action plan" to deal with specific procrastinations.

III. POSSIBLE ACTIVITIES:

A. 1. Use the following, or one of your own, as an example to illustrate the concept:

Things I put off doing	Feelings as a result	Is it really a priority?	Action Plan
the laundry	unproductive and guilty	☑ yes ☐ no	I will do one load every other day!

   2. Encourage group members to complete handout and facilitate discussion.

   3. Process benefits of positive time management skills.

B. 1. Brainstorm with group members tasks most often delayed or left undone and list on chalkboard.

   2. Encourage each member to choose one from the board (not their own) and give a possible action plan (perhaps one that has been successful for them in the past).

   3. Encourage group members to complete handout and facilitate discussion.

   4. Process benefits of positive time management skills and request that each group member share one action plan that he or she will begin.

COAT of ARMS

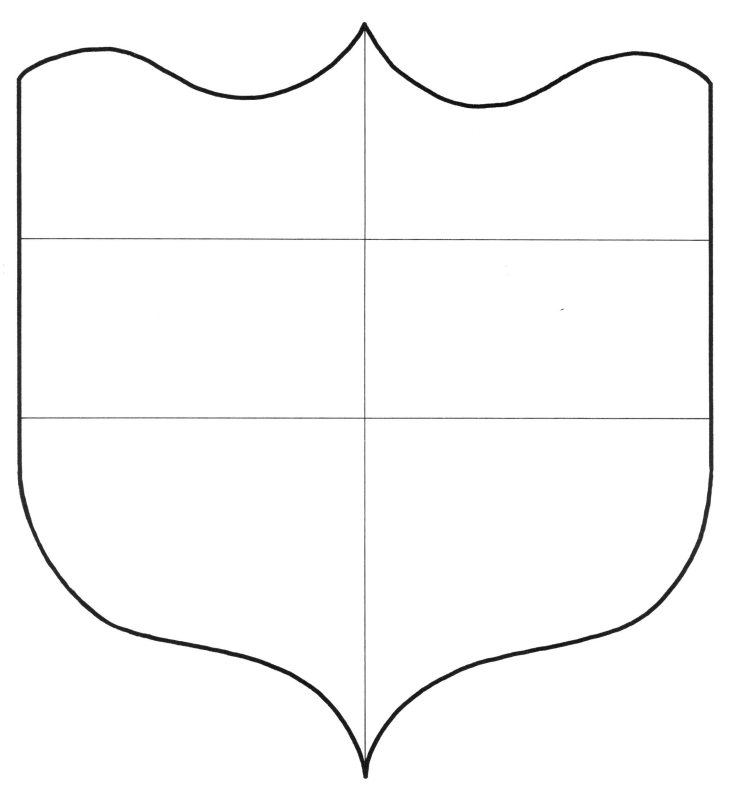

COAT OF ARMS

I. PURPOSE:

To increase values clarification and self-awareness.

II. GENERAL COMMENTS:

Identifying and clarifying values and expressing them honestly can facilitate self-awareness and allow for more open relationships. This handout is purposefully unstructured enabling a wide variety of values to be explored.

III. POSSIBLE ACTIVITIES:

A. 1. Supply a list of six or more possible topics that can be drawn, written, or symbolized in the blank boxes, e.g.:
Things I do well …
A turning point in my life was …
A low point in my life was …
Things I do poorly …
I'd like to stop doing …
A high point in my life was …
Something I value …
Things I'd like to do …
A peak experience I would like to have …

   2. Instruct group members to choose one topic for each box and complete the handout.

   3. Divide the group into dyads, giving five minutes for each to exchange information.

   4. Encourage dyads to rejoin group and share partner's "coat of arms" with group.

   5. Process benefits of this activity.

B. 1. Choose 6 topics that would be most appropriate for your group.

   2. Instruct group members to draw, write or symbolize their response to each topic.

   3. Encourage group members to explain their coat of arms.

   4. Process benefits of this activity.

Let's pretend - a friend

Male ☐ / Female ☐

Approximate age _____

Physical Appearance _____

_____

Personality / Beliefs / Values _____

_____

Other Special Talents / Interests / Abilities _____

_____

What would he / she offer you? _____

_____

What would you need from him / her? _____

_____

What would you offer him / her? _____

_____

Have you ever had anyone like this in your life? _____

Who? _____

Is there anyone in your life that could be this person? ____

Who? _____

If no, how could you go about finding this friend? _____

_____

Let's pretend -
a friend

I. **PURPOSE:**

To evaluate qualities and values of friends and friendships.

II. **GENERAL COMMENTS:**

Friendships are an important aspect of many people's lives. Recognizing the values one has regarding friends/friendship might enhance a more active approach to these relationships.

III. **POSSIBLE ACTIVITIES:**

A. 1. Brainstorm with group examples of each category in the two upper boxes and list on chalkboard, e.g., Physical characteristics — brown hair, shapely legs, tall, good posture.

2. Instruct group members to complete their handout referring to chalkboard as needed.

3. Encourage group members to complete the bottom box individually.

4. Facilitate discussion of responses.

5. Process benefits of evaluating potential friends/friendships.

B. 1. Discuss role of friendships in people's lives.

2. Instruct group members to complete handout.

3. Collect handouts and read aloud one at a time encouraging group members to guess the author of each.

4. Summarize as a group what action each will take as a result of this activity.

What DO I Value ?

The degree to which we live by our own sense of values can greatly influence our self-satisfaction. When we say we hold a specific value in high regard, yet act in a manner which opposes this value, inner conflict can result.

List below your 5 highest values and note how they are *expressed* in your life and / or how they are *opposed*.

I value:	I *express* this by:	I *oppose* this by:
Loyalty	Keeping secrets. Defending my friends.	Gossiping. Not being there when my friends need me.
Classical Music	I go to concerts and listen to tapes while driving.	Watching TV every evening after work instead of putting on my records.
1.		
2.		
3.		
4.		
5.		

What DO I Value ?

I. PURPOSE:

To promote values clarification by evaluating one's five highest values.

II. GENERAL COMMENTS:

Clarifying values allows one to know himself/herself better. Decisions can be influenced with developed insight and possible changes can therefore occur.

III. POSSIBLE ACTIVITIES:

A. 1. Discuss values clarification and present handout using description and examples provided at top of page.

2. Encourage group members to complete handout.

3. Facilitate discussion allowing each group member to present his/her most interesting example.

4. Process benefits of activity.

B. 1. Discuss values clarification and present handout using description and examples provided at top of page.

2. Encourage group members to complete handout.

3. Instruct each group member to (a) pantomime his/her five highest values with others guessing what they are; (b) identify one benefit from doing this activity.

These are the Topics in the Life Management Skills Book Series.

Life Management Skills I, II, III, IV, V & VI Topics	LMS I	LMS II	LMS III	LMS IV	LMS V	LMS VI	Total Handouts
• Abuse					3		3
• Activities of Daily Living		2		2			4
• Aging			2		2		4
• Anger Management		6					6
• Anxiety/Fear						3	3
• Assertion	4	3					7
• Body Image			2				2
• Combating Stigma				2			2
• Communication		4	3	2			9
• Conflict Resolution			2				2
• Coping Skills		4	4		8		16
• Coping w/Serious Mental Illness				3			3
• Creative Expression			2			5	7
• Discharge Planning	2						2
• Emotion Identification	2						2
• Exercise	3						3
• Feedback			2				2
• Goal Setting	4					2	6
• Grief/Loss		3			3		6
• Healthy Living			3			4	7
• Home Management				4			4
• Humor		2		2			4
• Independent Living Skills						3	3
• Interpersonal Skills					2	3	5
• Job Readiness			2	2			4
• Journalizing				3			3
• Leisure	2			4	4	2	12
• Life Balance		3					3
• Making Changes					4		4
• Medication Management					4		4
• Money Management		3					3
• Motivation	2						2
• Nurturance			4				4
• Nutrition	3						3
• Parenting		2		3	2		7
• Personal Responsibility						2	2
• Positive Attitude					2	3	5
• Problem Solving	3						3
• Recovery/Relapse Prevention		3	2		4	8	17
• Relationships			5	4	4	3	16
• Reminiscence		3					3
• Responsibility				3			3
• Risk Taking	3						3
• Role Satisfaction	2		4				6
• Safety Issues		2					2
• Self-Awareness	3		4				7
• Self-Empowerment			2				2
• Self-Esteem	4	3	2	2	4	2	17
• Self-Expression					2		2
• Sexual Health				2			2
• Sleep	2						2
• Social Skills			2	2			4
• Spirituality						3	3
• Stress Management	3	2	3	6		5	19
• Suicide Issues				2			2
• Supports	2	2			2		6
• Time Management	3	3					6
• Therapeutic Treatment						2	2
• Values Clarification	3			2			5
TOTAL ACTIVITY HANDOUTS	50	50	50	50	50	50	300

Use these card games to facilitate development of Life Management Skills! Each deck of cards covers the wide variety of topics in its corresponding book. Since there are more cards than required for a typical 50-minute group session, you can choose the specific topics and cards that would be most beneficial for your intended population and setting.

You can liven up groups with relevant topic cards. Teach by 'DOING'! Use these open-ended cards, integrating knowledge while playing a card game! Each deck of cards corresponds with one of the Life Management Skills books. In the lower right corner of each card is the page number of its corresponding book. Can be used alone or with corresponding books.

---

18 FOCUS TOPICS including: Discharge Planning, Emotion Identification, Goal Setting, Motivation, Nutrition, Problem Solving, Risk-Taking, Role-Satisfaction and more.

Here are some examples from 4 of the other topics:

VALUES CLARIFICATION: *What qualities do you value in the people you deal with regularly (honesty, loyalty, trust, sincerity, intelligence, etc.)?*

STRESS MANAGEMENT: *How do you presently cope with a difficult situation in your life? How can you improve your coping skills?*

SELF-AWARENESS: *When was the last time you truly felt good about yourself? What were the circumstances?*

ASSERTION: *Describe one way you can better communicate with someone important in your life.*

63 cards + 9 blanks to fill in your own!
(Corresponds with Life Management Skills I)

| PRDW-71011 Self-Manager I cards | $15.95 |

---

18 FOCUS TOPICS including: Communication, Grief and Loss, Life-Balance, Money Management, Parenting, Reminiscence, Steps to Recovery and more.

Here are some examples from 4 of the other topics:

TIME MANAGEMENT: *Can you be counted on to be on time? Why or why not?*

SUPPORT SYSTEMS: *Is it easy for you to accept help? Will you ask for help when you need it?*

ANGER MANAGEMENT: *What is something that sparks your anger? How do you handle it?*

SELF-ESTEEM: *When you are given a compliment, do you usually acknowledge or accept it? Do you suggest that you really don't deserve it?*

63 cards + 9 blanks to fill in your own!
(Corresponds with Life Management Skills II)

| PRDW-71012 Self-Manager II cards | $15.95 |

---

18 FOCUS TOPICS including: Aging, Body Image, Conflict Resolution, Creative Expression, Feedback, Healthy Living, Nurturance, Self-Empowerment and more.

Here are some examples from 4 of the other topics:

COPING SKILLS: *Have you ever used "writing" . . . writing letters, journal writing, or poetry - as a way to learn more about yourself or to cope with stress? If yes, describe. If no, would you try?*

RELATIONSHIPS: *Do you feel fatigued after spending time with a certain friend or relative? Who and why?*

JOB READINESS: *What are 3 benefits of women working outside of the home?*

SOCIAL SKILLS: *What is a label, stereotype, or prejudice that offends you? Why?*

63 cards + 9 blanks to fill in your own!
(Corresponds with Life Management Skills III)

| PRDW-71013 Self-Manager III cards | $15.95 |

---

18 FOCUS TOPICS including: Activities of Daily Living, Serious Mental Illness, Relationships, Responsibility, Sexual Health, Suicide Prevention/Awareness, Values and more.

Here are some examples from 4 of the other topics:

COMMUNICATION: *Name 3 topics that you can talk about with someone you've just met. What are 3 things not to talk about with someone you hardly know?*

JOURNALIZING: *I have learned _____ about my mood/illness/health.*

HUMOR: *Name 3 things, or people, that always make you laugh.*

STRESS MANAGEMENT: *How long do you tend to hold on to anger or hurt feelings? How do you let go?*

63 cards + 9 blanks to fill in your own!
(Corresponds with Life Management Skills IV)

| PRDW-71014 Self-Manager IV cards | $15.95 |

---

15 FOCUS TOPICS including: Coping Skills, Grief, Interpersonal Skills, Leisure, Parenting, Positive Attitude, Self-Expression and more.

Here are some examples from 4 of the other topics:

MEDICATION MANAGEMENT: *What are "over-the-counter" medications for? Compare them with prescription medications.*

RECOVERY: *What are symptoms of your illness that warn you when it may reoccur?*

ABUSE: *If someone asks you to go out with them and your intuition tells you not to, what can you do and say?*

MAKING CHANGES: *What are 3 unhealthy eating habits you have?*

63 cards + 9 blanks to fill in your own!
(Corresponds with Life Management Skills V)

| PRDW-71015 Self-Manager V cards | $15.95 |

---

15 FOCUS TOPICS including: Goal Setting, Healthy Living, Personal Responsibility, Positive Outlook, Relationships, Self-Esteem, Spirituality and more.

Here are some examples from 4 of the other topics:

ANXIETY/FEAR: *Finish the sentence: I am fearful of _____. Explain.*

EXPRESSIVE THERAPY: *If you were a 'super-hero' – what would two of your 'super-skills' be?*

INDEPENDENT LIVING SKILLS: *What benefits are, or would, be important to you in a job?*

THERAPEUTIC TREATMENT: *What role does 'trust' play in your Doctor/Patient relationships? How about your personal relationships?*

63 cards + 9 blanks to fill in your own!
(Corresponds with Life Management Skills VI)

| PRDW-71016 Self-Manager VI cards | $15.95 |

WELLNESS REPRODUCTIONS & PUBLISHING, LLC
A Guidance Channel Company

Call for catalogue 800 / 669-9208
or Fax 800 / 501-8120
e-mail: info@wellness-resources.com
website: http://www.wellness-resources.com

LMS I Order Form

SHIP TO:

First Name	Last Name	MI

Title or Initials	Department

Organization/Facility

Street Address	Suite or Apt. No.

City	State	Zip + four

Phone	Fax

E-mail Address

BILL TO:

First Name	Last Name	MI

Title or Initials	Department

Organization/Facility

Street Address	Suite or Apt. No.

City	State	Zip + four

Phone	Fax

E-mail Address

GUARANTEE: *Wellness Reproductions & Publishing, LLC stands behind its products 100%. We will refund, exchange or credit your account for the price of any materials returned **within 30 days** of receipt (excluding shipping).* **ALL MERCHANDISE NEEDS TO BE IN PERFECT, RESALE-ABLE CONDITION.** *Simply call us at 1-800-669-9208 for a return authorization number.*

Order Code	Quantity	Name of Product / Description		Page No.	Price Each	Total Price
PRDW-71001		Life Management Skills I book			$ 39.95	
PRDW-71011		Self-Manager I cards (corresponds with Life Management Skills I)			$ 15.95	
PRDW-71000B		KIT - Life Management Skills I book and cards (value $57.90)			$ 49.95	
PRDW-71000A		KIT - Life Management Skills I, II, III, IV, V and VI (value $247.70)			$219.95	
PRDW-71010		KIT - All 6 Self-Manager cards (value $95.70)			$ 79.95	
PRDW-71000		KIT - All 6 Life Management Skills books and cards (value $343.40)			$299.95	
PRDW-71156		EMOTIONS©	black & white laminated poster - 24" x 36"	(page 7)	$ 15.95	
PRDW-71217		FOOD FOR THOUGHT	black & white laminated poster - 24" x 36"	(page 22)	$ 15.95	
PRDW-71256		POSITIVE PROBLEM SOLVING	black & white laminated poster - 24" x 36"	(page 24)	$ 15.95	
PRDW-71216		DECISION MAKING	black & white laminated poster - 24" x 36"	(page 25)	$ 15.95	
PRDW-71283		TO RISK OR NOT TO RISK	black & white laminated poster - 24" x 36"	(page 27)	$ 15.95	
PRDW-71278		SELF-ESTEEM	black & white laminated poster - 24" x 36"	(page 37)	$ 15.95	

Method of Payment:
- ☐ Check or money order in U.S. funds.
- ☐ Purchase Order (must be attached) P.O. #_____
- ☐ Visa *VISA*   ☐ MasterCard *MasterCard*   ☐ American Express *AMERICAN EXPRESS*

Subtotal	
Shipping and Handling	
Subtotal	
NY and OH Sales Tax	
Grand Total	

Account Number | Expiration Date | Signature _____

See below for Shipping/Handling information.

5 Easy Ways to Order:

To expedite all orders include order code above.

① **CALL us Toll-Free:**
1/800/669-9208

② **SEND us:**

Wellness Reproductions & Publishing, LLC
P.O. Box 760
Plainview, NY 11803-0760

③ **FAX us Toll-Free:**
1/800/501-8120 WRPI

④ **ORDER ONLINE:**
http://www.wellness-resources.com
(with credit card - **secured**!)

⑤ **EMAIL:**
info@wellness-resources.com

SHIPPING/HANDLING

*REGULAR GROUND:

Add 8% (min. $5.95) in 48 contiguous states.

For Alaska, Hawaii, Puerto Rico, Canada and all other international locations; and for rush, express or overnight delivery, please call for rates and delivery information.

Shipments outside of the United States may be subject to additional handling charges and fees. Customers are responsible for any applicable taxes and duties.

*CANADA:

Orders may be sent to Wellness Reproductions and Publishing, LLC, or call for a distributor in your area.

Our Order Policies ensure fast, efficient service!

SALES TAX: New York and Ohio residents, add sales tax on total, including shipping and handling. Tax-exempt organizations, please provide exempt or resale number when ordering.

SHIPPING: Every order, including small orders, will receive our best service. However, a minimum charge of $5.95 shipping and handling must be added to offset the cost of processing the order. Please provide complete street address including suite or apartment number.

TERMS: Purchase orders, net 30 days F.O.B. NY. All international orders must be **prepaid in U.S. Funds.**

PRICING: Prices effective July 1, 2001. This order form supersedes all previous order forms. Prices subject to change without notice. If this form has expired, we will bill you any difference in price.

UNIVERSITY INSTRUCTOR? If you are considering using this book as a school text or supplemental resource, please call our office to discuss desk copies and quantity education discounts.

METHODS OF PAYMENT:

Check: Make your check payable to Wellness Reproductions & Publishing, LLC.

Purchase Order: Mail or fax a purchase order. Be sure to include name of person using products, title, and department. Include signature of person placing order.

Credit Card: Please include account number, expiration date and signature.

UPDATE OUR MAILING LIST: You are automatically added to our mailing list when you order your first product from us. If you want to change your address, remove your name, or eliminate duplicate names from our file, please contact us. Until we correct our duplicate mailing, please pass along an extra copy of this catalogue to one of your colleagues.

PROBLEMS? WE'LL TAKE CARE OF THEM! Call us immediately if you have any questions about your order.

OUR IRONCLAD GUARANTEE:

We guarantee your complete satisfaction. You may return any product within 30 days for immediate refund or credit.

Please photocopy, complete and mail to Wellness Reproductions and Publishing, LLC, P.O. Box 760 • Plainview, New York 11803-0760

FEEDBACK - LIFE MANAGEMENT SKILLS I

1. Check the topics that were of special interest to you in LMS I.

_____ Assertion	_____ Motivation	_____ Self-Esteem
_____ Discharge Planning	_____ Nutrition	_____ Sleep
_____ Emotion Identification	_____ Problem Solving	_____ Stress Management
_____ Exercise	_____ Risk Taking	_____ Support Systems
_____ Goal Setting	_____ Role Satisfaction	_____ Time Management
_____ Leisure	_____ Self-Awareness	_____ Values Clarification

2. What topics would be of interest in future publications?

a) _____

b) _____

c) _____

3. Which were your favorite handouts?

a) _____

b) _____

c) _____

4. Describe an activity that you have created for any of the pages in this book.

_____

_____

_____

If this activity can be published in our WELLNESS NET•WORK newsletter or website, please sign with your professional initials for publication. If it is selected, you will receive a $25 WELLNESS gift certificate.

(signature) _____

5. Comments on LMS I: _____

_____

_____

Can these comments be published?   _____ Yes   _____ No

(signature) _____   *(date)* _____

Name _____   Title _____

Facility _____   Occupation _____

Address _____   Home Address _____

City _____   City _____

State _____ ( ) _____ Zip _____   State _____ ( ) _____ Zip _____

Phone (work) _____   Phone (home) _____

email _____   Fax _____

(SEE REVERSE SIDE FOR ORDER FORM)

FOR OFFICE USE ONLY: Order # _____   Date _____

SHIP TO:

First Name | Last Name | MI

Title or Initials | Department

Organization/Facility

Street Address | Suite or Apt. No.

City | State | Zip + four

Phone | Fax

E-mail Address

BILL TO:

First Name | Last Name | MI

Title or Initials | Department

Organization/Facility

Street Address | Suite or Apt. No.

City | State | Zip + four

Phone | Fax

E-mail Address

GUARANTEE: *Wellness Reproductions & Publishing, LLC stands behind its products 100%. We will refund, exchange or credit your account for the price of any materials returned **within 30 days** of receipt (excluding shipping).* **ALL MERCHANDISE NEEDS TO BE IN PERFECT, RESALE-ABLE CONDITION.** *Simply call us at 1-800-669-9208 for a return authorization number.*

Order Code	Quantity	Name of Product / Description		Page No.	Price Each	Total Price
PRDW-71001		Life Management Skills I book			$ 39.95	
PRDW-71011		Self-Manager I cards (corresponds with Life Management Skills I)			$ 15.95	
PRDW-71000B		KIT - Life Management Skills I book and cards (value $57.90)			$ 49.95	
PRDW-71000A		KIT - Life Management Skills I, II, III, IV, V and VI (value $247.70)			$219.95	
PRDW-71010		KIT - All 6 Self-Manager cards (value $95.70)			$ 79.95	
PRDW-71000		KIT - All 6 Life Management Skills books and cards (value $343.40)			$299.95	
PRDW-71156		EMOTIONS©	black & white laminated poster - 24" x 36"	(page 7)	$ 15.95	
PRDW-71217		FOOD FOR THOUGHT	black & white laminated poster - 24" x 36"	(page 22)	$ 15.95	
PRDW-71256		POSITIVE PROBLEM SOLVING	black & white laminated poster - 24" x 36"	(page 24)	$ 15.95	
PRDW-71216		DECISION MAKING	black & white laminated poster - 24" x 36"	(page 25)	$ 15.95	
PRDW-71283		TO RISK OR NOT TO RISK	black & white laminated poster - 24" x 36"	(page 27)	$ 15.95	
PRDW-71278		SELF-ESTEEM	black & white laminated poster - 24" x 36"	(page 37)	$ 15.95	

Method of Payment:

☐ Check or money order in U.S. funds.

☐ Purchase Order (must be attached) P.O. #_____

☐ Visa **VISA**   ☐ MasterCard   ☐ American Express

Account Number | Expiration Date | Signature _____

Subtotal	
Shipping and Handling	
Subtotal	
NY and OH Sales Tax	
Grand Total	

See below for Shipping/Handling information.

5 Easy Ways to Order:

To expedite all orders include order code above.

① CALL us Toll-Free:
1/800/669-9208

② SEND us:

Wellness Reproductions & Publishing, LLC
P.O. Box 760
Plainview, NY 11803-0760

③ FAX us Toll-Free:
1/800/501-8120

④ ORDER ONLINE:
http://www.wellness-resources.com
(with credit card - secured!)

⑤ EMAIL:
info@wellness-resources.com

SHIPPING/HANDLING

*REGULAR GROUND:

Add 8% (min. $5.95) in 48 contiguous states.

For Alaska, Hawaii, Puerto Rico, Canada and all other international locations; and for rush, express or overnight delivery, please call for rates and delivery information.

Shipments outside of the United States may be subject to additional handling charges and fees. Customers are responsible for any applicable taxes and duties.

*CANADA:

Orders may be sent to Wellness Reproductions and Publishing, LLC, or call for a distributor in your area.

Our Order Policies ensure fast, efficient service!

SALES TAX: New York and Ohio residents, add sales tax on total, including shipping and handling. Tax-exempt organizations, please provide exempt or resale number when ordering.

SHIPPING: Every order, including small orders, will receive our best service. However, a minimum charge of $5.95 shipping and handling must be added to offset the cost of processing the order. Please provide complete street address including suite or apartment number.

TERMS: Purchase orders, net 30 days F.O.B. NY. All international orders must be **prepaid in U.S. Funds.**

PRICING: Prices effective July 1, 2001. This order form supersedes all previous order forms. Prices subject to change without notice. If this form has expired, we will bill you any difference in price.

UNIVERSITY INSTRUCTOR? If you are considering using this book as a school text or supplemental resource, please call our office to discuss desk copies and quantity education discounts.

METHODS OF PAYMENT:

Check: Make your check payable to Wellness Reproductions & Publishing, LLC.

Purchase Order: Mail or fax a purchase order. Be sure to include name of person using products, title, and department. Include signature of person placing order.

Credit Card: Please include account number, expiration date and signature.

UPDATE OUR MAILING LIST: You are automatically added to our mailing list when you order your first product from us. If you want to change your address, remove your name, or eliminate duplicate names from our file, please contact us. Until we correct our duplicate mailing, please pass along an extra copy of this catalogue to one of your colleagues.

PROBLEMS? WE'LL TAKE CARE OF THEM! Call us immediately if you have any questions about your order.

OUR IRONCLAD GUARANTEE:

We guarantee your complete satisfaction. You may return any product within 30 days for immediate refund or credit.

FEEDBACK - LIFE MANAGEMENT SKILLS I

1. Check the topics that were of special interest to you in LMS I.

____ Assertion	____ Motivation	____ Self-Esteem
____ Discharge Planning	____ Nutrition	____ Sleep
____ Emotion Identification	____ Problem Solving	____ Stress Management
____ Exercise	____ Risk Taking	____ Support Systems
____ Goal Setting	____ Role Satisfaction	____ Time Management
____ Leisure	____ Self-Awareness	____ Values Clarification

2. What topics would be of interest in future publications?

a) _____

b) _____

c) _____

3. Which were your favorite handouts?

a) _____

b) _____

c) _____

4. Describe an activity that you have created for any of the pages in this book.

_____

_____

_____

If this activity can be published in our WELLNESS NET•WORK newsletter or website, please sign with your professional initials for publication. If it is selected, you will receive a $25 WELLNESS gift certificate.

(signature) _____

5. Comments on LMS I: _____

_____

_____

Can these comments be published? _____ Yes _____ No

(signature) _____ *(date)* _____

Name _____ Title _____

Facility _____ Occupation _____

Address _____ Home Address _____

City _____ City _____

State ____ ( ) Zip ____ State ____ ( ) Zip ____

Phone (work) _____ Phone (home) _____

email _____ Fax _____

(SEE REVERSE SIDE FOR ORDER FORM)